The
Way
of the
Stick

Also in this series

IAIDO – The Way of the Sword

The Art of Shuriken Jutsu

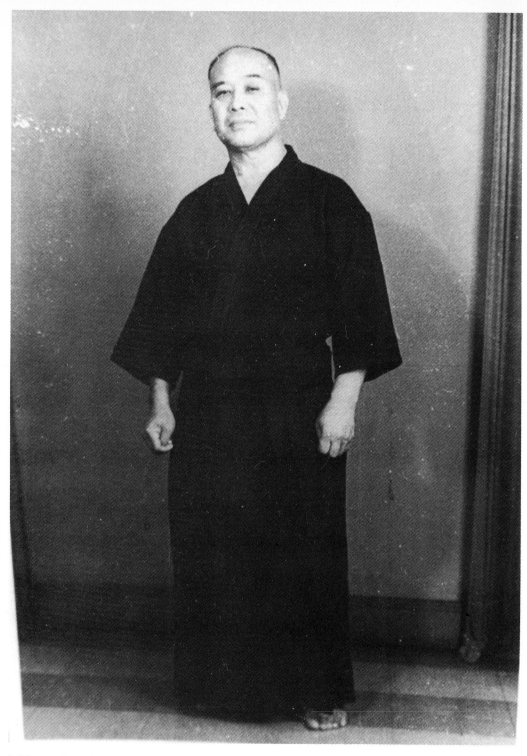

Ichitaro Kuroda Sensei, the leading authority on Shindo Muso Ryu Jodo, awarded the Emperor's Medal for contributions to the martial arts and the author's present teacher. Kendo 7th Dan, Kyoshi; Iaido 7th Dan Kyoshi; Jodo 8th Dan Shihan; Shodo 8th Dan Shihan.

The
Way
of the
Stick

MICHAEL FINN

Paul H. Crompton Ltd.
638 Fulham Road
London SW6
England

1st edition 1984

Acknowledgements:
I wish to offer my sincere
thanks to
Hiroko Kawanishi
for all her help
past and present.

I.S.B.N. 0 901764 728
Printed by Elsworth Printers Ltd., Leeds LS11 9DB.

Dedicated to the memory of the late Donn F. Draeger Sensei.

CONTENTS

FOREWORD

This book is an introduction to the way of the stick, it is however no ordinary system but the essence of a style that is over 300 years old, called Shindo Muso Ryu. The stick has been used in many nations over many generations as a weapon of defence; in the Ming dynasty of China, in Japan, on Okinawa and in Great Britain where it was called the Quarter Staff. No system has attained such cultural, historical or practical note in modern times as Shindo Muso Ryu Jodo.

The stick system of Shindo Muso Ryu was designated in Japan a National Cultural Treasure by the emperor. It is a system from which the Japanese Riot Police (Kidotai) developed their system of police stick training. It is the system of stick accepted by the Japanese Boy Scouts for their staff training. Shindo Muso Ryu Jodo has followers in every part of the world. It not only develops combative spirit but helps us to deal calmly with any situation. This system is the only one that has been accepted by the All Japan Kendo Federation, who grade in its representative techniques 'Jodo Seitei No Kata'.

Within these pages you will find everything you need to give you the knowledge and background of Jodo Seiteigata (when seitei and kata come together they are pronounced seiteigata). We cover the History, Cultural background, Philosophy, the twelve Kihon (Basic Techniques) and the twelve Kata (Training Forms). The book is laid out in a practical and easy to follow manner and is the first of its kind in the English Language. It is a must for the library of the serious Martial Arts exponent.

ABOUT THE AUTHOR

Michael Finn is a well known authority on Martial Arts and has written numerous books and articles both in Britain and abroad. He began his Martial Arts studies in 1957 at the age of twelve and has continued his training ever since.

At the age of twenty-one he joined the Metropolitan Police Force and two years later became National Police Judo Champion. In 1968 Michael went to Japan for two years intensive training under Japan's foremost teachers in Martial Arts, during that time he represented Britain in the World Kendo Championships.

On his return to Britain he joined the City of London Police and instructed them in self defence. In 1974 he left the police force to found his own Elite Martial Academy, where study and research in numerous Martial Arts are made. Since leaving the force Michael has been instructor and advisor for many national bodies including the Metropolitan Police, City of London Police, Royal Marine Commandoes, American Military Police, American Forces, and many Private Schools.

Michael has 30 black belts in nine different Martial Arts which include Judo; Kendo; Iaido; Jodo; Nunchaku; Rokushakubo; Sai; Tonfa and Aikido. All these grades are recognised by the respective Japanese governing bodies. Apart from this he is a qualified Shiatsu practitioner and authority on some of the more obscure aspects of Martial Arts, which include Shuriken Jutsu.

In respect of Shindo Muso Ryu Jojutsu, Michael was one of the few foreigners to be graded by the last grand master of Shindo Muso Ryu Jojutsu, Takaji Shimizu dai sensei. This book displays his dan ranking certificate. In respect of Kendo Remmei Jodo Seitei no Kata, Michael holds Shodan as well. He has held these grades for the last 13 years in continued practice.

Some of Michael Finn's qualifications:

British Judo Association .... 1st Dan
Kodokan Judo Institute .... 1st Dan
All Japan Jodo Federation .... 1st Dan
Shindo Muso Ryu Jojutsu .... 1st Dan
All Japan Kendo Federation .... 2nd Dan
All Japan Iaido Federation .... 2nd Dan
Muso Shinden Ryu Iaido .... 3rd Dan
Tomiki Aikido .... 3rd Dan
Japan Karate Do Itotsuki Ryu Nunchaku .... 4th Dan
Japan Karate Do Itotsuki Ryu Rokushakubo .... 4th Dan
Japan Karate Do Itotsuki Ryu Sai .... 4th Dan
Japan Karate Do Itotsuki Ryu Tonfa .... 4th Dan
Certified Namikoshi Shiatsu Therapist (Japan)

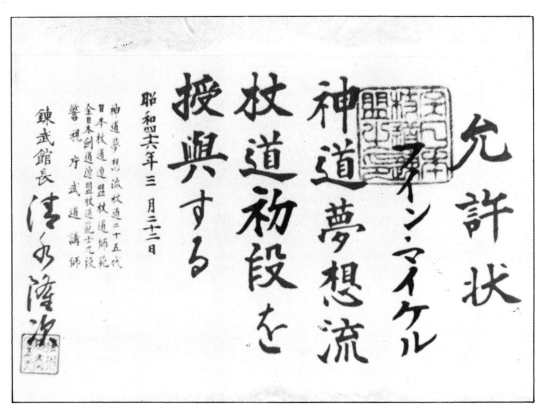

Black Belt Certificate awarded to Michael Finn by Takaji Shimizu Dai Sensei.

INTRODUCTION

Shindo Muso Ryu Jojutsu was a system that developed in Japan's feudal era. The strategy and techniques of the school were very difficult to learn and for many years were taught in secret. Because of the complexity of Jojutsu it never became popular in the same way that Kendo, Judo and other sport forms did just after the Meiji restoration, about 1868.

The teachings of Shindo Muso Ryu Jojutsu were imparted only to the few who came for dedicated study. However, because there is so much benefit from its training it was decided by the All Japan Kendo Federation, under the direction of the 25th Grand master Takaji Shimizu Dai sensei, to bring its teachings within the grasp of the general public. In the original system there were 64 kata and 12 kihon. From this was developed a system of 12 kihon and 12 kata that would express the underlying principles of the Ryu.

We will in later chapters deal with the background and history of the Shindo Muso Ryu but for the moment some introductory information may be of interest. The system was developed about the beginning of the 17th century by Muso Gonosuke Tokichi, who defeated the famous swordsman Miyamoto Musashi. Apart from the Jo, the system also includes Kusarigamma of Isshin Ryu, Tanjo of Muso Ryu, Jutte of Ikkaku Ryu, Hojojutsu of Ittatsu Ryu and Kenjutsu of Shinto Ryu. In these respects it is a complete school of Martial Arts.

The Jo is a versatile weapon because of its simplicity. It can be used to thrust, sweep, strike or block and both ends can be used with the same ease. The combative strength of Jo is that the enemy can be taken by surprise. He will not realise its effectiveness until it is too late. This will allow you to find a weak point or an unguarded moment. The jo is not intended as a killing weapon and this is another part of its value; the spirit of the Jo is in its use to chastise.

The Jodo Seitei of the All Japan Kendo Remmei has been matched so that it complements modern society, as with Jigoro Kano and his Judo maxim 'minimum effort and maximum efficiency', so does the same maxim apply to Jodo.

The author in Japan with Shimizu Dai Sensei, the 25th Grand Master of Shindo Muso Ryu.

7

It is a skill that can be studied by all ages and all sexes and is becoming popular not only in Japan but throughout the world.

Apart from its more obvious attributes the skill of Jodo rests in intuitive rather than intellectual understanding. There are no empty hand techniques as all training includes the use of the Jo, but the training is a balance of spiritual and physical discipline and is based on many aspects that transcend words. The training is called 'Ishin Denshin' (direct transmission) and from this the following become component parts that are often neglected in the Western world:

Training aspects of Jodo

1. Reigi 'Dojo etiquette'; Shingi 'faith'; Seijitsu 'Honesty'; Shisso 'Simplicity'.

2. The above are aspects that develop you internally in the spiritual sense and are complemented by; Shinsei 'Posture'; Taido 'Attitude'; it is these that develop you physically (Externally). All of these things will go towards Fukaku 'Good Character'.

3. Ketsuden Ryoko 'Decisive Ability' and Handan Ryoko 'Judgement' are qualities that develop confidence.

The techniques in Jodo are the method by which to find the way and are not a means in themselves; the future study of Jodo and its development depend on training with Honesty, Integrity and Sincerity.

I personally trained for two years with the grand master Takaji Shimizu Dai Sensei in Shindo Muso Ryu Jojutsu and also in the Kendo Remmei Jodo Seitei no Kata and was graded to black belt rank in both systems at separate exams, during my stay in Japan. In the twelve years since that time I have never been able to return and take another exam but I have continued training in Britain, Switzerland and America. I am sure my knowledge will be put to good purpose and have tried to collate it as exactly as possible.

The Author Michael Finn.

PERSONAL ANECDOTES IN JAPAN

I remember when I first went to Japan twelve years ago the one thing I had always wanted to study was Jojutsu. On my arrival I asked if there were any places that taught Jo but everyone got it confused with either Kendo or Naginatado and I was told it did not exist.

One day I attended the Kagamibaraki 'New Year Festival' at the Nihon Budokan, where a special demonstration of Martial Arts was taking place. It was there I met Quintin Chambers, who was also from Britain, and had been in Japan about eleven years. When I asked him if he knew of any school that taught Jo, he told me he had heard something about one. From that point he asked me a lot of questions about myself and suggested I phone him early one morning the following week and he would look for the dojo address.

I had to get up early that morning anyway, about 6 a.m., because I had an early class in Aikido, so I phoned Quintin. He told me he had not found the address and asked me to phone back early another morning. This process went on for quite some time but I was still no nearer to finding a Jo dojo. Then one morning he suggested I come over to his house and that he may be able to help me in my search.

I went to Quintin's house one weekend and after a meal we went out for a drink and a chat. We spoke quite deeply about a full range of subjects and before I left he said that if I met him one day the following week, he would take me to the Jo dojo which was in Tomisaka.

Foreign students who trained with Shimizu Dai Sensei. From the top left of the photo: Paul Maloney, Nigel Jackson, Ed Martinez, the Author Mike Finn. Bottom row from the left: Press reporter, Quintin Chambers, Shimizu Dai Sensei and Donn F. Draeger Sensei.

On the appointed day I met him and we walked up a hill with wooden fronted shops in Japanese design. We turned down the side of a police station and in a little backyard was an annexe of slatted wood, weather worn and in shabby condition. The door to the annexe was ill-fitting and almost fell off as Quintin opened it. Inside were some Japanese and Western people in Hakema. The room was a small dojo with wooden floor, worn by constant use; above in the beams of the ceiling hung many Kendo armours.

Quintin went up and spoke to an elderly man, small in stature even by Japanese standards. He had very expressive eyes, that seemed almost to replace words, and through his humility shone tremendous charisma. Later I found out that he was Takaji Shimizu Dai sensei. Quintin also spoke to a man whom I only recognised through books; it was Donn Draeger whom I later came to know well and corresponded with until he passed away last year. He was the world's foremost authority on Martial Arts and had forgotten more than most men knew on the subject. I was informed by Quintin that it would be possible for me to train in the dojo, and I went home elated.

When I first went to the dojo I was taught one technique; each lesson lasted from three to four hours and at first I was left in a corner with my one technique, while everyone got on with their training. I was more or less ignored for quite some time, then one day everyone suddenly seemed to notice me still there and my tuition began in full. I was later told that the Ryu was not for everyone and the first thing to be established was how keen I was. This explained all the questions and the early morning phone calls. The long period with one technique was also part of the test to gauge my tenacity and interest. I am sure my character was also under close scrutiny.

One day shortly after the training session I was given a big bag in which all the Jo were stored. Draeger sensei asked me to hold it open so everyone could put their Jo inside, but placed the bag so it was over my feet. I just clicked in time as the first Jo was being put in and moved my feet. Everyone laughed as this was the usual trick for beginners. As they hold the bag everyone tries to score a hit on the foot as their Jo goes in. I do not know if I passed or failed the test but it certainly kept me on my toes in the dojo from that time on. It was always hard to tell a joke in the dojo because everyone was so good at keeping a poker face.

My Japanese was never very good so I could only use simple sentences. I was always impressed how well Shimizu Dai sensei could communicate with me. He was perhaps the person who was the biggest single influence on my approach to Martial Arts and Ways. When Shimizu Dai sensei taught he never wasted anything. He would never teach a new technique until I had competence in the previous technique. He knew exactly which stage all his students had reached so no one could pretend to have learned more than they really had. His techniques were very effective, without the slightest sign of effort being used. He was certainly the Grand Master. I consider myself lucky to have had the honour of studying under him.

11

Both Donn Draeger and Quintin Chambers were senior black belt ranks in the dojo and present at almost every session, and a great help to me in my studies. Both spoke fluent Japanese. In the modern system of Jodo attention is not paid to the Heiho (strategy) of the older combative system, but Draeger sensei took the time to show me both ways of training which gave me a clearer insight into how the modern system developed. He also was a person who had his own charisma, and was completely involved in the study of Martial Arts. If you were to take all his grades and total them the number would be well over a hundred black belts in various skills, but such skill and dedication cannot be measured in that manner.

I remember on one occasion after an afternoon training session we all went to a nearby restaurant, where we used to talk about Martial Arts and kindred matters over a coffee and a snack. I had just ordered a coffee and an egg sandwich and Donn Draeger had decided to have a creme caramel. The rest had various other things. When Donn Draeger's creme caramel arrived in a tall dish on a plate we all stared in amazement; it was almost microscopic. At this point most people would have complained bitterly to the management, but not Donn Draeger, he picked up the large dessert spoon he had been given and said to us "Hell, it will be gone in one mouthful if I use this". He called the waiter over and asked him if he could have a teaspoon instead, so his creme caramel would last longer.

The Rembukan was the old dojo, it was in Omori on the outskirts of Tokyo and the honbu (head dojo) for Jodo. In the summer you could walk along some of the backstreets to it and imagine the old Japan. The backstreets were narrow, with no pavements and wooden houses either side. In the small gardens with bamboo trelliswork stood Matsu (pine) and Kiri (Paulownia). In Japan's feudal era when a daughter was born to a household, they would plant Kiri in the front garden. The Kiri grows very quickly and would be quite large when the girl was of marrying age. When the girl got married it would be cut down and furniture made of it for her dowry. It was also a sign to eligible young men, that a young girl of marriable age lived in the house. It was knowing these anecdotes that created the atmosphere and charm during my walk to the dojo.

The dojo itself was one of character. It could for all appearances be transported from Japan's feudal era. Its wooden framework was warped with the weather and bore the character of a dojo that had been used with austerity and frugality. Inside the dojo was a well worn wooden floor and ill fitting sliding windows that let the elements in during the winter months to test your endurance. The roof was high with interlacing wooden beams, but the unforgettable feature of the dojo was its toilet. In a small room with a rickety sliding door and an almost stable floor, was the toilet, a hole about 1' 6" in diameter that looked down to a chemical pit some ten feet below. It was a remnant of a bygone age. In the summer months it supplied the dojo with a memorable aroma and in the winter an endurance test that defied all others, when a ritual visit was made.

The Rembukan Dojo, Headquarters of Shindo Muso Ryu Jojutsu.

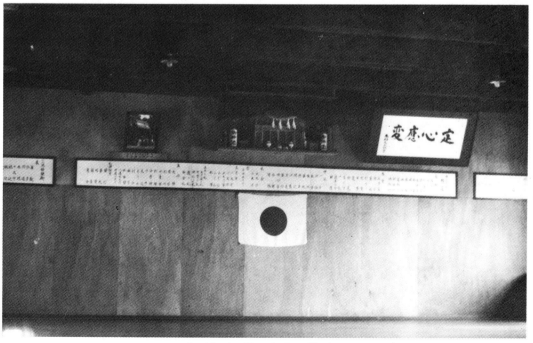

Inside the Rembukan Dojo.

Kuroda Sensei and Shimizu Dai Sensei together during a national demonstration of their skills.

There were many memorable tales of the Rembukan dojo. I remember one summer about eight of us were training in the dojo and Kuroda sensei was giving instruction. I am sure those who train in Jo will know the technique called Hikiotoshi; it is used when the attacker makes a challenge and holds the sword in chudan (middle position). The Jo exponent strikes the sword with his stick, at such an angle that it can be wrenched from his hands. To achieve this takes years of dedicated training and skill. As we were all busy training in our respective techniques, Kuroda sensei did Hikiotoshi on his opponent, with such power that it tore the sword from his hand. It went the length of the dojo past us, through the open window and into the park beyond. We all spend the next half hour, still in hakema, searching the shrubbery to recover the bokken. Then we returned to the dojo to continue training.

In Jo there are few accidents but when they do occur, they often are apt to be serious. At an examination for Seitei Jodo, having taken part and completed what was required, I was watching the other exponents. Two students were performing Ranai, which is a long kata. At the end of the kata the Jo man strikes down with the stick and the sword man steps back and separates his hands to avoid the strike (this section has been changed a little since that time). Then the sword man joins his hands again at the sword and cuts at his opponent. In this instance as the sword man separated his hands, he glanced over to look at his girl friend who was watching from the side. In that fraction of a second he misjudged the timing and instead of stepping back, walked into the end of the jo, which ripped open his forehead and stripped the flesh from the bridge of his nose. He fell to his knees with blood pouring from the wound; everyone rushed up to help him but no one had anything to put on the injury. The Dutchman who was next to me reached into his bag and produced a towel, which I think had been there for the past six months, and apart from the pungent smell it looked a little rigid with continual use. He handed this to the injured person who used it to staunch the bleeding, after that he was whisked off to hospital. I expect he survived both the injury and the pre-hospital treatment.

In the evening after a training session I returned to my small flat, or perhaps it more resembled a large cupboard. It was important to remember and train in my Jo techniques, so I used to practice in the narrow street outside the flat. At about 10 p.m. all the local residents used to go to the public baths at the end of my road; custom in Japan was quite casual so the women would walk along the street in a nightdress or dressinggown and the men in pyjamas. They all had with them little bowls and face flannels. On my first evening of my training session I was not aware of them and unknown to me they had all congregated some distance up the street, thinking that perhaps I had escaped from a local institution. I wondered why I had the street to myself.

As I continued my Jo training a neighbour who knew me could see what was happening. She came over and told me that some people would like to get through to take a bath. When I looked up the street there were about 30 people in pyjamas, holding bowls and looking very worried. She went up and explained I was a 'henna gaijin' (foreigner). This seemed to supply them with a complete answer, and they replied, "Oh, a foreigner, well, that explains it". My neighbour explained that I was training and after that they used to pass me on their way to the bath, and say 'good evening'.

I remember on my journey back to Britain which took 3 weeks via the Trans Siberian Express, I used to go through the Jo movements in the compartment, of course without the Jo. Since then there has never been a week gone by when I did not do regular practice, in all the Martial Arts I studied.

One day in the Rembukan dojo I was training with Pascal, who is now a senior teacher of Jodo in Switzerland, whom I introduced to the dojo. There were only the two of us and Kuroda sensei was giving instruction, while we were doing a technique called Midare, in which you spin the stick on its axis to strike down the sword. As I spun the stick the end of it came up and smashed me in my left eye. There was blood trickling down my face, but it was not correct form to stop until the technique was completed. As I continued the technique I noticed there were some of my eyebrows stuck on the end of my Jo, which did not make me feel any better about it. I imagined that at least my eye must be hanging on my cheek, but could not tell because of the blood. At last the technique was completed.

A demonstration of Naginata (left) and Yari (right). Two weapons from which the movements of Jojutsu originated.

I went straight to a mirror to have a look. All it was, seemed to be a small deep cut over my left eye, which did not look much at all after the blood was wiped away. Kuroda sensei explained that he had been expecting me to make that mistake for some time, but felt that had he told me I may not have taken the same notice as finding out for myself. Believe me when you find out by experience, you never forget. Kuroda sensei then gave me some interesting first aid. He got me to hold a big wad of cotton wool over the eye while he ran a long piece of tape from my forehead to my lip. We continued the training session, but when I got home I removed the dressing as it gave the impression I had undergone major surgery. A small plaster was put on instead.

There are many anecdotes I could talk of but this book is about Jodo, so they have all been Jodo related. There was so much I understood by being with the grand master; the concept of learning by direct transmission is very important in traditional Martial Arts training. There are experiences and moments where no words have been exchanged, but by the events themselves much has been understood. As these things are beyond words, of course I cannot write about them, but by relating some of the stories an insight may be possible; if you have felt as well as read these pages then you will understand what I try to convey.

JOJUTSU HISTORY

The 20th century marks the development of the 'Do' system but even today the old traditions prevail.

The staff has been a weapon used throughout Japan's history and is even recorded in the 'Nihon Shoki' (early records). The feudal era has seen the development of hundreds of schools in stick fighting, using a whole variety of sticks. The Bo was usually about six feet in length; the Hanbo was about three feet in length; the Jo was about four feet in length; the Hananegi was a very short stick; the Tetsubo was a long staff made of iron or with iron strips and studs on it; the Hakabuko was an eight sided staff and the tanjo was also a short staff of about three feet. There were many other types of stick but the above define a few of the main types.

The Japanese staff was normally made of Kashi or Kashiwa (both various types of oak). This is about the most suitable wood to use. The Japanese oak has a high water content which gives it weight, the grain is very close which prevents splintering and it is resilient enough to have just a little but not too much give in it. In the traditional manner the oak was cut and dried naturally, it was turned at intervals over a period of years, so that it was well seasoned. In modern times the wood is kiln dried, which often deprives the wood of too much water too quickly. There still are in Japan a couple of people who make Jo in the traditional manner. In real training it is not just a simple matter of using any old bit of wood.

17

Many ryu had within their system the use of some kind of staff. There was Kongishi Ryu founded by Matsuoka Masachika; Katori Shinto Ryu founded by Izasa Choisai; Takeuchi Ryu bojutsu; Muhi Ryu; Kiraku Ryu; Araki Ryu; Kyoha Ryu; Yoshin Ryu; Ryusei Ryu; Kashima Shin Ryu; Ryusei Shingan Ryu; Kukkishin Ryu and of course Shindo Muso Ryu. Most Ryu had as their core weapon the katana, but Shindo Muso Ryu has as its core weapon the Staff.

Before we look into the history of Shindo Muso Ryu Jojutsu it is important to know about Mount Homan in Kyushu, as without a background knowledge of this mountain the tradition would make little sense. The national religion of Japan is Shintoism which is pantheistic. God is in all things and even mountains possess a character or spirit, and this is the case with Mount Homan.

The mountain is 868 metres high and has a very unusual rock formation. It is a mountain that has a feeling of spiritual quiet, much like the grounds of Glastonbury Abbey in Somerset Britain; the resting place of the legendary King Arthur. The mountain was not however always a spiritual place, at the time of Jimmu Tenji (662-671) it was a mountain that brought bad luck to many. Because of the character of the mountain the emperor directed that a ceremony be held to remove its evil spirit. This was done by invoking the god Hyugoshin (a god of protection who kept away demons). After that time the mountain became a religious one, the emperor Temmu Tenno (673-686) had a shrine built on the mountain. The shrine was Reiho Homanzan Kamakado Jinja and was dedicated to the mother of Jimmu Tenno, the first emperor. The shrine was for his earthly mother and not the sun goddess Amaterasu no Mikami.

In the time of Temmu Tenno a famous priest called Shinren Shonin of the Sohoshu sect climbed Mount Homan and built a monastery called Hochuji. In the Taiho Jidai (701) it became a very popular place of worship and in 802 a famous Buddhist Priest called Denkyo Taishi (Saicho) went to the mountain to pray for the safety of a merchant ship sent to China, called Kento Sen. After that Denkyo Taishi built a temple called Aritomo Yammatera and in 818 built a temple annexe called Hoto, where sacred relics were kept. After that over 370 Hermitages were built, but in later years they and the temple were destroyed by fire. However, about 1000 Jizo (statues) still remain.

The word 'Ho' means treasure, but not in the sense of buried gold. It means the more intangible treasure of a more beautiful nature. 'Manzan' means the complete mountain so we may call 'Homanzan' treasure mountain. The mountain is also reputed to be haunted by 'Tengu' (mountain demons). They have long noses and are supposed to be expert swordsmen. The book 'Tengugeijitsuron' is an account of their strategy in swordsmanship. From the above account you can see the religious and martial influence that exists within the borders of this mountain.

Jo dimensions:
Length = 4 Shaku - 2 Sun - 1 Bu
(50¼inches approx).
Diameter = 8 Bu (1 inch approx)
Type of wood – Kashi or Kashiwa
(Japanese Oak).

The founder of Shindo Muso Ryu Jojutsu was Muso Gonosuke Katsuyoshi and the history of the Ryu began over 300 years ago. Muso Gonosuke studied for many years at Tenshin Shoden Katori Shinto Ryu, a school that was responsible for the original stem of many Ryu that had been founded after the teacher had gained knowledge from this, the oldest, extant school in Japan. Gonosuke stayed with this school until he became qualified and received his certificate from the master.

Muso Gonosuke then studied Kashima Shin Ryu, the founder of which was Matsumoto Bizen no Kami. One of his specialities was the study of Ichi no Taito (a thick sword) and he remained with this school until the Keicho era (1596). It was from these two schools that he began to formulate his own ideas and concepts.

19

About 1596 Gonosuke became a Mushashugyo (a warrior who trained in many dojo, to try out his skill). He had many encounters during his travels but was never defeated. During the Keicho era there was another master who was never defeated and who won such renown that it carried his name even through to modern times. That man was Miyamoto Musashi Kuronobu, who wrote the book of strategy called Go Rin No Sho (Book of Five Rings) and was famous for his use of the two-sword style.

According to tradition these two men met to test their skills and in the ensuing encounter Gonosuke was defeated. Gonosuke was using a Rokushakubo (six foot staff) and probably much of the strategy of Katori Shinto Ryu, but he came up against Musashi's strategy of using Juji Dome. Musashi as far as can be ascertained through various accounts, caught the Rokushakubo in the angle of his two crossed swords and trapped it there. The encounter was not fatal but Gonosuke was advised never to return to try his skill.

After this encounter Gonosuke travelled to the southern islands of Japan called Kyushu and came to rest in Fukuoka, in Chikuzen no Kuni. During this time he is said to have trained with the Yama Bushi and gained extra skill; of the fact he retreated to the mountains there is no doubt.

Gonosuke ended his search for a way in which to defeat Musashi and get past the technique of Juji Dome, when he went to meditate at mount Homan. He meditated there for a period of 37 days at a shrine and one night while he was asleep, a small boy came to him in the form of an angel. The boy imparted to him certain secret teachings that today are the centre of the System and are still secret. The boy advised him to use a stick of the length 4 shaku 2 sun and 1 bu with a diameter of 8 bu. This meant that the stick was long enough to keep the swordsman at bay, but allowed greater mobility than the longer Bo.

When Muso Gonosuke awoke he formulated the movements for his system, based on the striking action of the sword, the sweeping action of the naginata (halberd) and the thrusting action of the spear. After perfecting his technique Gonosuke again returned to challenge Miyamoto Musashi. With the weapon called the Jo, given to him by the divine providence of Homanzan, Gonosuke encountered and defeated Miyamoto Musashi. The encounter was not fatal and Musashi recognised the genius of this young warrior. The two later became well acquainted and Musashi introduced him to the Kuroda Han in Fukuoka where he became Instructor in Jojutsu of the style Shindo Muso Ryu. The words themselves explain the importance Homanzan had on his teachings; 'Shin' means god or god spirit and is sometimes pronounced 'Kami', the word 'Do' means a path or direction, the way to be followed and is sometimes pronounced 'Michi', the word 'Muso' means a dream or vision and is of course the prefix of Gonosuke's name, and the word Ryu is a collection of Martial Skills within a school. The meaning of Shindo Muso Ryu should now have a clearer meaning.

Shindo Muso Ryu Jojutsu was kept a secret of the Kuroda Clan (Han) for centuries. The 25th lineal descendant in the line of Grand Master was Takaji Shimizu, who died about eight years ago. His teacher was Suenaga Setsu, and while Shimizu Dai Sensei was in his youth he was directed to leave Fukuoka and introduce Jojutsu to Tokyo. The first demonstration he gave was in 1931 in Kyoto and from there he went to Tokyo and at the request of Jigoro Kano, the founder of Judo, began to teach Jojutsu at the Kodokan (Judo headquarters) in Suidobashi.

Jigoro Kano spoke about Jojutsu and related it to Judo; one aspect of Judo is for protection, however an attacker often uses a weapon. In many situations there is always a stick handy, particularly in the home. Most families have at least one stick about the house and with the skill of Jojutsu people could protect themselves, even against a sword. In this way Judo and Jojutsu both complement each other. As a result of Jigoro Kano having such foresight, he invited Shimizu Dai Sensei to join him and teach stick. Shimizu Dai Sensei taught there from 1932 until 1945.

Another well known figure in the Master's life was Nakayama Hakudo, who was the 16th Grand Master of Muso Shinden Ryu Iaijutsu. He said it was through the study of Shindo Muso Ryu, during his youth, under Uchida Ryogoro, that he understood the 'Kendo no ura' (hidden meanings of Kendo). During his kendo practice he used the hand and footwork from Jojutsu and the hip movement, and found them very effective. At a demonstration in the Butokukai in Kyoto during a national meeting of Shindo Muso Ryu he said of Jojutsu, it was like 'Koku Ho Teki' (A national treasure). Those words were prophetic because in 1970 Takaji Shimizu Dai Sensei was awarded by the Emperor of Japan, the title of 'Living National Cultural Treasure' for his Jojutsu.

In 1953 Jojutsu was accepted as part of the All Japan Kendo Remmei along with Iaido and Naginata. Twelve years later the first Jojutsu dojo, called the Rembukan, was established in Tokyo and by that time the police, the boy scouts and the youth groups had all accepted Jojutsu as part of their training system. Today the riot police are all instructed in this style of stick training under Tsunemori Kaminoda. Jojutsu has, through Shimizu Dai Sensei, been introduced throughout the world and helped towards international friendship.

Because of its complexity, in the early days, Jojutsu was not as popular as other skills. To popularise Jo and encourage people to study it, the techniques which numbered 64 Kata and 12 Basic movements that were called Kihon, were studied and simplified. The All Japan Jodo Federation under the All Japan Kendo Federation and the direction of Shimizu Dai Sensei, introduced the twelve Kihon from Jojutsu and Twelve selected Kata from Jojutsu. The kata were in some cases altered from those of the Ryu, to make them more understandable.

21

This system called Jodo has become very popular among Kendo exponents who want to understand a little more about older systems, and has grown throughout the world.

I would like to make it quite clear to the reader at this stage that there is a vast difference between Shindo Muso Ryu Jojutsu and the All Japan Jodo Federation's Jodo. The Jojutsu is a classical school of stick that is practiced in a traditional form and retains the format and character of the Ryu. Its repertoire of techniques not only include the 12 Kihon and 64 Kata but also encompass other weapons; Shinto Ryu Kenjutsu; Muso Ryu; tanjojutsu; Isshin Ryu; kusarigamma; Ikkaku Ryu; jutte jutsu and Ittatsu Ryu, hojojutsu. These are respectively, Sword, Short stick, Sickle and chain, Iron truncheon, and Rope tying technique. Although in recent years black belt ranking has been awarded for these skills, in earlier days only certificates of competence would be awarded at various stages, the first being 'Okuiri', and awarded about the grade of 4th dan. This is Shindo Muso Ryu Jojutsu.

The All Japan Kendo Federation introduced through the All Japan Jodo Federation, a system called 'Jodo' and based on the teachings of the Shindo Muso Ryu. It is a simplified and independent concept from the above Ryu. The All Japan Jodo Federation is composed of the following: a series of warming up exercises using the Jo; Four basic postures; Twelve basic uses of the Jo and Twelve forms. All black belt examinations are based on the above format.

This book explains the techniques of the All Japan Jodo Federation. It is not meant as a teach yourself book because even with simple and easy to follow photos and text, much will be lost. It is a reference book for those who are Martial Arts Exponents and want to expand their general knowledge of the subject, and for those who already study or intend to study this system and wish to use it as a guide to complement their regular class.

THE JO

The exact size of the Shindo Muso Ryu Jo is 4 shaku, 2 sun and 1 bu, in Japanese measurement. The diameter of the Jo is 8 bu. To translate this to British measurement one 'shaku' would be about one sixteenth inch shorter than a foot, the 'sun' would be about one and a quarter inch, and the 'bu' would be about one eight of an inch. The overall length of the Jo would be about 50¼inches and the diameter would be about 1 inch. In Japanese measurement there are 100 bu; which equal 10 sun and 10 sun equal 1 shaku, which means there are ten Japanese divisions per shaku, and twelve British divisions per foot. This comparative variation means that although the shaku is shorter than the foot, the sun is longer than the inch.

The Jo is made of Kashi or Kashiwa as I have explained, which is Japanese oak. There are very few substitutes that meet the correct requirements for Jo. The same Jo is used for Shindo Muso Ryu Jojutsu and for Seitei Jodo. The Bokken is also of Japanese oak. You should **not** put anything such as linseed oil on the Jo or Bokken (wooden sword), or varnish it in any way. If you do this it will impair the use of the weapon. The weapons will eventually become impregnated with the natural oils from your hand, if you train regularly.

Remember when you get your Jo and Bokken it is not just any old stick; it is your weapon of training. Treat it with the respect of anything that you have to rely on and which will serve you for perhaps all your training days. Don't leave it lying around for others to pick up and use. Always remember your Jo, even if it does not have your name on it. The Jo will have each mark of blood and sweat on it, from every training session you ever had, and in time, if you cannot tell your Jo from a hundred thousand then a part of your training is missing.

JODO GI

The usual clothing worn for training is a Hakema (divided and pleated trousers) and the Haori (Kimono type jacket). The Hakema is normally blue but can be brown, white or black. There are three pleats on one side and two on the other. The Haori is normally blue, ties at the chest and is loose weave fabric.

The Haori is put on first, then you step into the Hakema and bring the front up to the waist. The two long tapes at the front go around the back, cross over at the front, then tie in a bow at the back. The back of the Hakema lifts up and rests at the top of the buttock, the two rear tapes come around and tie up at the front. There are several ways of wearing the Hakema; often the front is tied with a special knot. The Jo may well catch in such a knot, which is more suitable for funerals and weddings. This also applies to the securing of the Haori. If tied in a bow the Jo may get caught in it, then suddenly free itself and smash you in the face. This type of incident can hurt. It is better to tie a simple knot.

Wearing the Hakema.

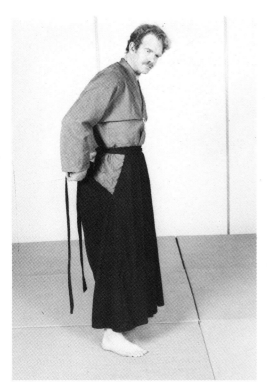

When carrying your training clothing with you, it is better not to take them off and just stuff them in your bag. Not only does this make them creased, but the next time you train it may give those around you the impression you thrive on being scruffy. Your training relies on self-discipline and this is reflected in your approach to training. Care of your kit is as important as the training itself. There are various ways to fold a kit. This is one of them. Move the flap on the inside of the Hakema to the left, then lay the Hakema down with the front uppermost. Lay out all the pleats neatly and fold the tapes across the upper part of the Hakema. Fold the hard pad of the Hakema under and both the sides of the Hakema inwards. When this is done fold the Hakema over, into a smaller size. This is an informal way but neat. The formal manner is rather complex.

Lay out the Haori face upwards, place the folded Hakema in the centre of the Haori. Fold the arms into the chest, over the Hakema and then fold the outside parts of the jacket inwards over the Hakema. Lift up the lower part of the Haori and bring it up to the top, then place the kit in your bag.

Folding the Hakema.

JODO SEITEI NO KATA TECHNIQUES

Below are listed the bowing, basic postures, kihon, kata and basic exercises.

1. REI: (Bowing)
    Zarei — Sitting Bow
    Ritsurei — Standing Bow
2. SHISEI: (Posture)
    Ritsu Jo — Standing Posture
    Sage Jo — Carrying Posture
3. KAMAE: (Preparatory Posture)
    Tsune No Kamae — Basic Posture
    Honte No Kamae — Basic Starting Posture
    Gyakute No Kamae — Reverse Posture
    Hikiotoshi No Kamae — Side Posture
4. KIHON: (Basic Techniques)
    Honte Uchi — Basic Strike (Right/Left)
    Gyakute Uchi — Reverse Strike (Right/Left)
    Hikiotoshi Uchi — Side Strike (Right/Left)
    Kaeshizuki — Thrust (Right/Left)
    Gyakutezuki — Reverse Thrust
    Makiotoshi — Winding Sweep
    Kuritsuke — Sword Trap
    Kurihanashi — Sword Spin
    Taiatari — Sword Avoid and Push
    Tsukihazushi Uchi — Sword Strike and Thrust
    Dobarai Uchi — Block and Strike Down
    Taihazushi Uchi — Avoid and Strike (Right/Left)

    (The translations into English are not literal but practical)

5. JODO SEITEI NO KATA:
    Tsukizue — Reaching Stick
    Tsuigetsu — Sternum Thrust
    Hissage — Withdrawing Stick
    Shamen — Side Head Strike
    Sakan — Left Thrust with Sword
    Monomi — Lookout Technique
    Kasumi — Poor Sight Technique
    Tachiotoshi — Sword Strike Away
    Raiuchi — Thunderbolt Strike
    Seigan — Aiming at The Eyes
    Midaredome — Stopping Disorder
    Ranai — Disorder to Harmony

(The above translations are somewhat more literal, but some may not make too much sense on face value.)

When translating the meanings of techniques from Japanese to English, it is important to realize that often the words have no sensible meaning in everyday Japanese conversation. The words are technical in much the same way that 'A big end' would mean something to a car mechanic, or a 'Paramecium' would mean something to a biologist. Often technique names suggest the original inspiration for the technique, are a guide to what it is about, or just a tag to indentify it.

It is important that we know these Japanese names for techniques as this is the universal language for such Martial Arts studies and in retaining that tradition we keep its cultural values as a complete whole. The translation is a matter of conjecture, but provided we know what the Japanese term refers to and are capable of perfecting that technique then an important criterion rests there.

REI

The formal bowing in Shindo Muso Ryu Jojutsu at the beginning and the end of the Kata is not the same as that of Jodo Seitei no Kata. In Jodo there is a formal sitting bow and a standing bow which follows the pattern of modern budo.

ZAREI (Sitting Bow)

Uke and Tori approach each other until they are about six feet apart, which is a distance from which neither can reach the other without giving away his intention. Both sit in seiza at the same time, uke transfers his bokken to his right side, with the cutting edge facing away from him and the hilt level with his knee.

Tory sits in seiza facing uke and places the Jo to his right side, with the centre of the Jo about level with the centre of the upper leg, that is with about a foot and a half protruding past the knee. At the same both exponents face each other with their hands resting on their upper legs and with the backs completely straight.

After a pause both Uke and Tori slide their left hand from their knee to the floor and then in a simultaneous action both slide the right hand to the floor. The forearm and the hand should form a triangle, with the hands as the apex. With the back straight, both Uke and Tori bow to each other but at the same time ensure they can see each other's actions with peripheral vision. After a pause they both rise up together, sliding the right hand on to the leg first and then the left hand. Both pick up their respective weapons, stand up and retreat.

A

B

C

RITSUREI (Standing Bow)

Both exponents come towards each other and stop about six feet apart. Uke holds his sword in his left hand with the thumb on the tsuba (guard), the sword is held low at his side and not on the hip. The right hand is held straight but not rigid, at Uke's right side.

Tori on approaching Uke lowers his Jo from Tsune no Kamae to Sage Jo. His left hand is at his left side and the Jo is held in his right hand. Both Uke and Tori bow from the hip and keep their backs and heads in a straight line, as they do so. In Japan it is a mark of respect to bow lower than your superiors; that means that if you are working with a teacher of much higher grade, you would be expected to bow lower than him.

D

E

SHINSEI (Posture)

Posture is a cornerstone of Martial Arts studies; how you stand and walk will affect the manner in which you perform your techniques. Your back and head must always be in line so that your body is always in line with your centre of gravity. Your weight must be evenly distributed and concentration of your centre of gravity must be kept low.

RITSU JO

This posture should be adopted when you are standing still, perhaps listening to instruction. It prevents everyone in dojo doing different things with their Jo and retains the discipline and harmony of the class.

The Jo is held in the left hand and you are standing in normal posture, with your feet together and back straight. The right hand is relaxed at your right side and the Jo is by the left toes, in line with your body. The left hand supports the Jo, which is resting on the ground, by holding it at the centre so the arm is relaxed at the side and not bent to secure a grip on the stick.

A

SAGE JO (Carrying Posture)

In this posture the Jo may be held in either the left or right hand, it is a way in which to walk with the Jo so you do not knock into things or fellow students as you walk.

If you were holding the Jo in the position of Tsune no Kamae then your left hand would have the correct grip on the Jo, with the palm facing inwards and the knuckles facing outwards. The Jo is lowered so that the back end of the stick comes to rest behind the shoulder blade, the other end of the stick points towards the floor. Your other hand is kept resting at your side.

The Jo has been taped on one end; this is not traditional; it is so that you can tell which end has been used, in the photos.

B

A

KAMAE (Preparatory Posture)

There are four Kamae that you will need to understand and learn, before you move on to the Kihon. These four Kamae are component parts of the Kihon and serve as a framework for its understanding.

TSUNE NO KAMAE (Basic Posture)

Before you start each Kihon you will assume this posture; you must always be aware because it is in this posture that your opponent will approach you. Stand with your feet together and your body straight, your left hand is at the left side. The Jo is held in the right hand and there is a very slight bend in the right arm. The Jo should be held about the centre, but so that there is no strain on the part of your wrist and hand, as you are holding it. You must find the exact spot at which to hold the Jo without effort. It is not exactly the same for everyone. The Jo should be pointing upwards, in the direction of the point between your opponent's eyes. Do not grip the Jo either too tightly or too loosely.

HONTE NO KAMAE (Basic Starting Posture)

Most of the Kihon begin with Honte no Kamae; it is used to prevent the swordsman from getting into range of your body with the blade. As he approaches you will move into Honte no Kamae.

Start in Tsune no Kamae, raise the Jo forward and in a straight line towards a point between the centre of the eyes of your attacker. Do not allow the angle of the Jo to change. With beginners the tip of the Jo often drops a little as it is raised. This is wrong. As the Jo comes forward so you step one pace forward with your right foot and grip the end of the Jo with your

B   **C**

left hand, keep the Jo extended forward towards your opponent and do not hold it into your body.

If you are taking up left posture then raise the Jo forward with your right hand but step forward with your left foot. As you do this the left hand holds the Jo above the right and the right hand slides down the Jo to grip it at the end. In both cases the Jo must be held at the very end, so no Jo protrudes beyond the hand. The space between the two hands, while holding the Jo, should be about 14 inches but not too close that the weight of the Jo is felt or too high up so that you lean forward to grip it. The arms should not be too straight and the armpits should have a little space under them.

D

E

GYAKUTE NO KAMAE (Reverse Posture)

This is another posture that allows you greater versatility with the Jo. Stand in Tsune no Kamae, slide the left hand along the front portion of the Jo to the tip. The left hand secures the tip of the Jo with the palm facing inward and the knuckles facing the right. Now in a big overhead circular motion raise the Jo forward over the right side of the head, keeping the right arm fairly straight. At the same time step forward with the right foot and bring tip of the Jo to the point between the opponent's eyes. Now the left hand should be holding the end of the Jo in normal manner and the right hand should be holding the Jo in reverse. The right hand should be turned so the wrist is out and not in.

A

B

C

HIKIOTOSHI NO KAMAE (Side Posture)

Start in Tsune no Kamae; the left hand grips the end of the Jo in the same manner as before, except that the palm of the left hand is facing downwards. Now still holding the tip of the Jo bring the stick upwards to your left chest, so that the left palm faces outwards and holds the Jo loosely. At the same time step forward with the left foot so you are in an almost side-on position to the front. Let the right hand stay relaxed and slide down the Jo, taking a normal grip just over half way down the Jo. Ensure that your left elbow is kept into your body.

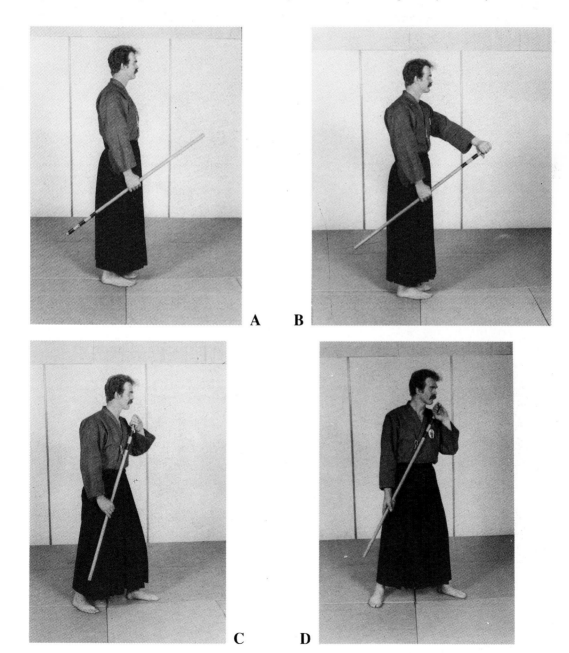

A   B

C   D

KIHON

基本

Kihon can be practised in either tandoku (single form) or sotai (pair form). In single form the students stand in line and the senior student will give the command. The students move from one side of the dojo to the other, repeating the technique. At the end the senior will shout Yamae (stop), then he will call out Motoe (lower the Jo) and Mawari Migi (turn right). You will turn to face the way you came and are ready to continue the next technique. At the end of the Kihon he will say Kihon Owari (Basic Technique Finished).

KIHON (Sotai Renshu)

本手打

HONTE UCHI:

Both exponents face each other about 12 feet apart, Uke holds the sword by his left side and Tori holds the Jo in Tsune no kamae, Tori lowers the Jo to Sage Jo and both exponents perform a standing bow to each other.

A

B

C

D

E

Uke raises the Bokken to his hip, draws the blade and steps one pace forward with his left foot into Hasso Kamae. Starting the first pace with his already advanced left foot, he walks towards Tori.

After the bow Tori right away raises the Jo to Tsune no Kamae and waits for Uke to approach. The Jo is longer than the sword so the initial movement must be made before Uke is within cutting distance.

Uke comes to Chudan Kamae at the same time as Tori raises the Jo to Honte no Kamae, the Jo should be pointing towards the centre point between Ukes eyes and the tip of the Jo and Bokken should be just crossing.

F

G

H

I

Uke lowers his Bokken and Tori, keeping his right hand exactly where it is, slides the Jo back with his left hand, until both ends are completely in the hand and not showing. Tori is going to make a strike to the centre of Uke's head so the ends of the Jo slide into the palms of both the left and right hands respectively. In this way you can change your grip by sliding both hands over the ends of the Jo. The left hand describes a big downward movement and at the same time Tori steps forward with his left foot and he strikes down with the Jo. To avoid the strike Uke steps back a pace out of range and Tori stops the strike about level with the eyes.

Tori keeps his left hand where it is and this time draws back the right hand. He repeats the strike on the other side, stepping forward with his right foot. Uke again takes a pace backwards.

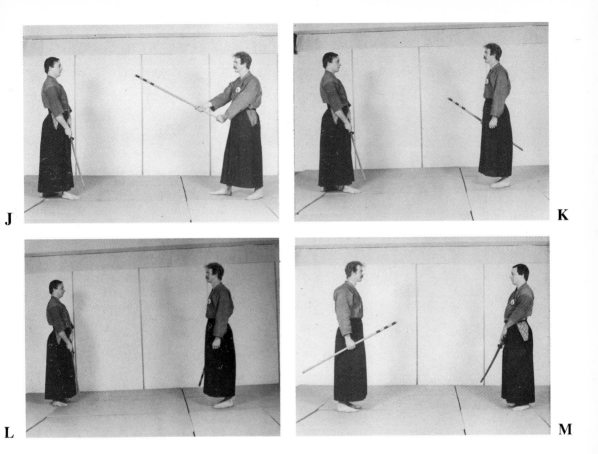

J

K

L

M

This sequence is repeated until both exponents near the end of the dojo, then Uke raises his Bokken after Tori's strike so that the Bokken and Jo cross at the beginning. There is a pause and Uke lowers his Bokken and takes a pace to his left side; when Uke's Bokken is lowered, Tori comes to Tsune no Kamae. If Tori is in right posture he releases the end of the Jo with his left hand, brings his left foot up to his right and allows the Jo to go to his right side. If he is in left posture he slides the Jo down and through the left hand to the tip, then as he brings the right foot up to the left, so the right hand slides half way up the Jo to Tsune no Kamae on the right side, the left hand goes down to the left side. When Uke steps to the left, Tori lowers the Jo to Sage Jo.

When the above action has been completed, Uke and Tori walk forward so that Tori is in Uke's position and Uke is in Tori's position. Both are now ready for the next technique.

GYAKUTE UCHI: 逆手打

Uke goes to Hasso Kamae with his left foot forward and as he steps to chudan Kamae so Tori advances his right foot into Gyakute no Kamae and both sword and stick cross at the tip.

Uke keeps the Bokken where it is as Tori draws the Jo back with his left hand, to its full extension. Tori keeps his right hand where it is, the left hand makes a big downward strike to the right temple of Uke. As the strike comes down, Uke steps back with his right foot and blocks the strike with the Shinogi (Upper side) of the sword. Tori is still in Gyakute no Kamae in left posture, he draws the Jo back to its full extension, keeping the left hand where it is. Tori steps forward with his right foot this time, as he strikes down towards Uke's left temple. Uke steps back with his left foot and blocks to his left side, with the Shinogi of the sword. Tori continues to step forward striking in Gyakute Uchi, both on the right and left until Uke comes to Chudan no Kamae and the Jo and Bokken tips cross. At that time both change places in Ichi Kotae (Turning around) as they did for the end of the first technique Honte Uchi.

A

B

D

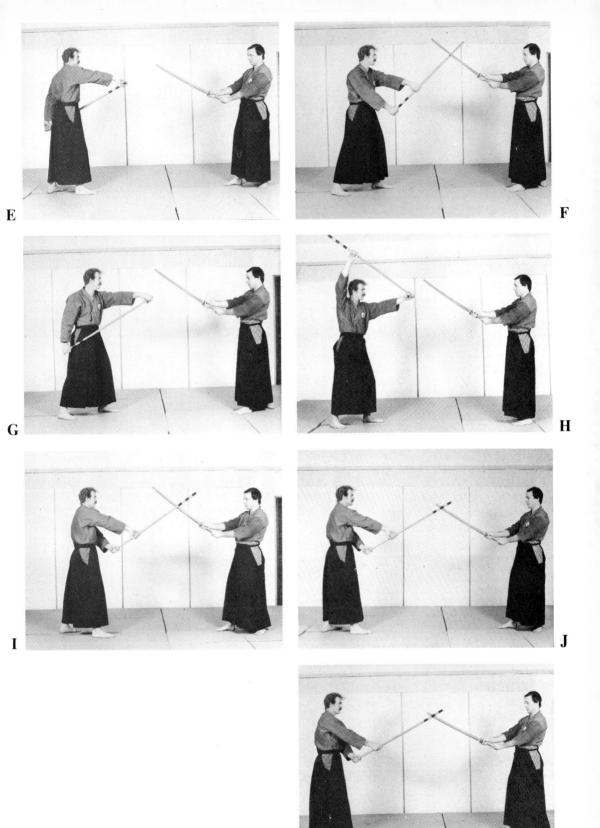

E

F

G

H

I

J

45

K

HIKIOTOSHI UCHI: 引落打

Uke goes to Migi Hasso no Kamae (right hasso) and the left foot is forward, from here he goes to Chudan no Kamae, advancing his right foot. As this happens, Tori goes to Hikiotoshi no Kamae. The advance to Chudan on the part of Uke is in the light of a challenge to Tori to act, he is not making a cut but just taking up a strong front.

Tori is going to sweep down the left side of Uke's blade (from the left as Uke looks at the sword) in a striking action, which is a very effective technique but is one that can really only be passed on by direct transmission from an experienced teacher.

Tori strikes the blade in Hikiotoshi no Kamae and advances his right foot a fraction of a second after the strike is initiated. The sword should be whipped back strongly to Ukes right side as it is struck, with the feeling that if it is not controlled it will be torn from his hands. To prevent this Uke steps back with his right foot and controls the Bokken as it goes back. Tori in the same movement as his strike, continues stepping forward with his right foot and brings the Jo up, pointing it between Ukes eyes.

Uke takes up right Chudan and at the same time Tori draws the Jo down into the palm on his left hand, reversing his grip by sliding over the end of the Jo. The Jo is pushed through the left hand until the other end is level with the chest and then the right hand changes grip and you are in Hidari Hikiotoshi no Kamae (left).

Uke is in Chudan so this time you are going to strike the right hand side of his sword, in the same manner you struck the left. This time you advance your left foot and come to his eyes, after the strike. As the strike is made to the right side of Uke's blade, he must pace back (not step) still in right posture and to take the force of the strike without letting go of the Bokken, the left hand crosses under the right as the blade is taken. Uke paces back and again brings the Bokken to Chudan no Kamae, Tori goes to Migi Hikiotoshi no Kamae and the technique is repeated until the end of the dojo is reached, at that time Uke brings up the Bokken and crosses the tip of Tori's Jo then they perform Ichi Kotae, and end up as before having reversed positions.

A   **B**

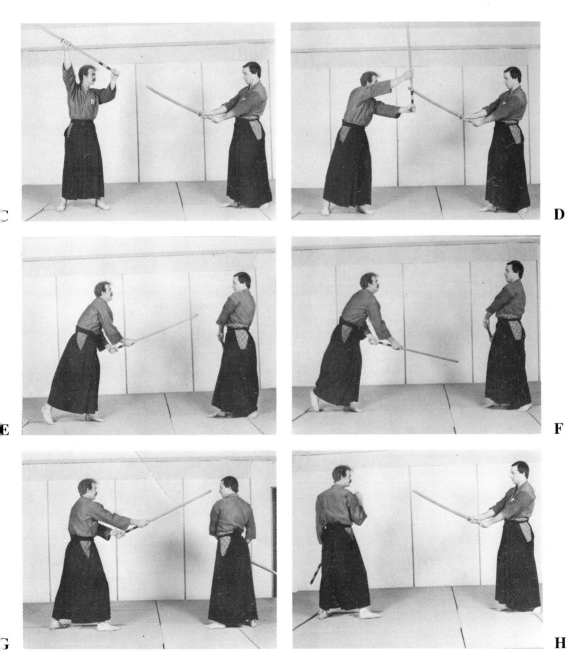

C

D

E

F

G

H

KAESHIZUKI: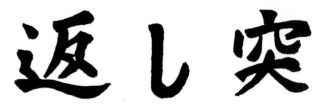

返し突

Uke and Tori face each other, Uke comes to Hasso Kamae and then to Chudan. As he comes to Chudan so Tori advances his right foot and comes to Honte no Kamae. Uke steps back with his right foot to Hidari Jodan no Kamae. Tori pivots on his right foot so it is facing outwards and the knee is facing outwards, at the same time he raises the Jo vertical sliding his right hand to the top of it. The left hand remains where it is but the ends of the stick are palmed by one hand at each end. The stick continues its journey through vertical, to a point parallel with the ground and directly behind Tori. At this point his hands have slid over the ends of the Jo and the left hand holds it palm up, while the right holds it palm down. Tori steps forward with his left foot and thrusts at Uke's solar plexus, then raises the Jo to cover his eyes.

A

B

C

D

48

E

F

G

H

I

Uke paces back and comes to Chudan no Kamae and crosses the tip of the Jo, again after a pause he steps back to Jodan no Kamae with his right foot. As he steps back to Jodan and not before, Tori pivots his left foot outwards and bends his knee outwards. The right hand remains where it is and the left hand slides up the Jo, which he raises vertically. Both hands slide to the ends of the Jo and this time it continues its journey through vertical, on the left side of the body ending as before. Tori now advances his right foot and thrusts to Uke's solar plexus, then covers the eyes. Uke again paces back to Chudan no Kamae and the technique is repeated, to the end of the dojo. In the end Uke is in Chudan no Kamae and just lowers his sword as a sign to Tori and both perform Ichi Kotae.

GYAKUTETSUKI:

Uke and Tori come to Chudan no Kamae and Honte no Kamae respectively and the Bokken and Jo cross. After a pause, Uke steps back to Jodan with his right foot. Tori at the same time pivots his right foot in the same manner as the last technique, but this time he keeps his left hand where it is and does not palm the stick. The right hand raises the stick directly above the head, so that Tori is looking directly along its centre. The right hand does not palm the Jo and both hands remain with the same grip on the stick.

A

B

C

D
E
F
G

Tori thrusts with the right hand at Uke's solar plexus and at the same time steps forward with the left foot. After the thrust Uke begins to step back with his left foot to Chudan but Tori, keeping the left hand where it is, draws the Jo back above the head with the right hand and stepping forward with the right foot strikes down in Honte Uchi to Ukes head. Uke retreats and blocks the downward strike on his left side, then adjusts his position to Chudan no Kamae crossing Tori's stick in Honte no Kamae.

This technique is only repeated on the right hand side so the above described action is continued to the end of the dojo, when Uke lowers his sword from Chudan no Kamae as a signal to Tori. Both perform Ichi Kotae.

52

MAKIOTOSHI:

Uke and Tori come to Kamae as before, Uke in right posture thrusts at Tori's throat. Tori paces back, still in right Kamae and slides his Jo along the inside of the Bokken, towards the tip. The Jo is at an inclination towards the left side and the hand grip remains the same. As Tori nears the tip of the Bokken, he scoops down and sweeps the Bokken to Uke's right side, paces forward still in right posture and brings the Jo up to Uke's eyes.

As the Jo sweeps away the Bokken, Uke steps back with his right foot and absorbs the impact of the sweep on his right side, then he brings the Bokken above his head and cuts for Jodan (head) advancing his right foot. Tori repeats the technique as before, drawing the Jo along the Bokken and dissipating the power of the cut, then doing Makiotoshi again on the right hand side.

A

B

C

D

From Uke's point of view the first attack is a thrust and thereafter is a cut. Tori continues his technique in the same manner on the right hand side all the way through. Both again end with Tori in Honte no Kamae and Uke in Chudan, with Bokken and stick crossed. Uke lowers the Bokken and both perform Ichi Kotae.

E

F

G

H

I

J

KURITSUKE: 繰付

Uke goes to Hasso no Kamae but Tori remains in Tsune no Kamae. After a pause Uke advances and cuts to Men (the head), as the cut comes down Tori steps to the left with his left foot and at the same time brings the Jo straight across his upper legs to his left hand and grips it at the end. The right foot of Tori steps forward and at the same time he brings the Jo upwards and the end goes between the two hands of Uke's descending Bokken, against the Tsuka. The Jo is now above Tori's head, the right forearm is level with the direction of the Jo. Tori now paces forward and at the same time pulls the Jo downwards, so that it traps Uke's hands and the sword to the front of his body. Tori holds the Jo against his upper legs to secure the technique, the left hand on the left leg and the right hand on the right leg.

A

B

C

D

56

Uke begins to step away from the hold that the Jo has on his wrists, as he does this Tori follows him with the end of the Jo which raises and focuses on the spot between the eyes. Tori is now in Kamae, with his right hand held in reverse on the Jo. Tori does not move the position of the Jo but changes the grip of the right hand from reverse to normal hold and then lowers the Jo to Tsune no Kamae, bringing the left foot up to the right. Uke now goes to Hasso no Kamae and the technique is repeated. When the end of the dojo is reached this time Uke does not come to Chudan no Kamae but simply does not raise the end of the sword to Hasso, then Uke takes a pace to the left, Tori lowers the Jo and advances and performs Ichi Kotae. This technique is only practised on the right.

E

F

G

H

I

KURIHANASHI:

Uke goes to Hasso no Kamae and again does not cross weapons with Tori, who remains in Tsune no Kamae. As Uke begins a cut at Tori's head, advancing his right foot as before, Tori again steps his left foot to the side and at the same time brings the Jo into his left hand. In a continuous movement he steps forward with his right foot and raises the Jo in the same manner as Kuritsuke, bringing the end of the Jo between Uke's two hands against the Tsuka (hilt). Uke still holding the Bokken, crosses his right hand over his left a little so the sword blade drops a little to his left hand side. The Jo is still in the same position on the Tsuka.

A

B

C

D

Tori paces forward and flicks the end of the Jo forward in a movement not unlike flicking oil from the end of the stick, and propels Uke's hands and Bokken in the direction he (Tori) is going. Uke paces of the force of the flick with several paces.

Uke faces Tori again and brings his sword to Hasso Kamae. Tori as before, changes his right hand grip on the Jo to normal position, still keeping the end of the Jo pointing towards Uke's eyes. Tori advances his left foot and lowers the Jo into Tsune no Kamae as the two feet come together. With Uke in Hasso no Kamae and Tori in Tsune no Kamae, both are ready to repeat the technique, which is only performed on the right. At the end of the dojo Uke again lowers the sword, pauses and takes a pace to his left, Tori then lowers the Jo, walks forward and both perform Ichi Kotae.

E

F

G

H

TAIATARI:

Uke faces Tori as before, in Hasso Kamae and Tori is again in Tsune no Kamae. Uke again cuts to Men and Tori responds as before by stepping to the left then forward, with the tip of the Jo between the Tsuka. At this point Uke brings his right foot back to his left and at the same time, raises his left hand above the left side of his head and the right hand above the right side. The blade is now parallel with the floor, above Uke's head, with the tip facing to the right. The Tsuka must be in front of the head and a little above it.

As Uke is going up to the above described position, so Tori turns his hips to face Uke and at the same time lowers his left hand so that it is in a position to punch at Uke's sternum. The right hand slides down the Jo so it is punching in the direction of Uke's face. The Jo is now vertical and the left hand is right at the lower end of the Jo. Tori paces forward and at the same time, keeping his arms straight, pushes Uke backwards. Throughout this action the hands have not changed their position on the Jo and as Uke moves backwards the Jo is lowered to the level of Uke's eyes. As before Tori now comes to Tsune no Kamae and Uke to Hasso no Kamae. At the end of the dojo Uke lowers his Bokken and steps to his left, Tori advances and they change around in Ichi Kotae.

A

B

C

NOTE:

In Kuritsuke, Kurihanashi and Taiatari the end of the sequence of each technique is not indicated by Uke bringing up his Bokken to cross the Jo, but by keeping the Bokken down and stepping to his left.

In Tandoku Renshu (single form practice) the techniques are repeated in a slightly different manner. After the first technique the exponent does not come to Gyaku then Tsune no Kamae, but simply repeats the application of the technique, until the end of the dojo, when he then comes to Gyaku and Tsune no Kamae to finish.

E

G

TSUKIHAZUSHI UCHI 突外打

Tori moves the stick across his body from Tsune no Kamae and grips the end with his left hand, and at the same time moves his left foot to the left. The Jo is raised above his head as the right hand slides to the other end of the Jo. The Jo is held parallel to the ground and above Tori's head, just a little in front of it. He remains in this stance.

A

62

B

C

Uke takes up Hasso no Kamae and slowly advances to Tori then as before, he pauses just out of range of the Jo. His left foot is forward and remains there, while he makes a slow action, drawing the Bokken as if cutting, across Tori's left shoulder to his right hip. This action is not an attack but a feint and the Bokken ends up at Uke's left hip. Uke now advances his right foot and at the same time thrusts the Bokken towards Tori's left side.

D

E

F

As the Bokken comes towards Tori he retreats side on, with his right foot forward and strokes the end of the Jo along the blade to deflect it. This is done with a drawing action which brings the Jo above the head, right hand in front and left hand behind the head. The Jo is on the same plane as the body but above the head and pointing downwards. Tori now releases the grip of the Jo with his left hand and turns his hips a little to his right, in this action he takes hold of the end which has just made contact with the Bokken and raises it a little to his right side, ready to make a strike. Tori strikes the Jo downwards with a sweeping action and knocks the Bokken back.

J

H

I

J

The Jo in the same movement comes to Uke's eyes and Tori takes a pace forward to drive him back, Tori then takes another pace forward and drives Uke back still further.

From Uke's point of view, after the Bokken has been struck down, he paces back at each thrust to his eyes.

K

L

Then Uke steps with his right foot, back into right Hasso Kamae, leaving the left foot forward. Tori raises the Jo above his head in the same manner he did in the beginning and waits for Uke to repeat his action. This technique is practised only on the right hand side, and continues to the end of the dojo. Uke steps forward with his right foot and comes to Chudan no Kamae, crossing the tip of Tori's Jo, then Uke lowers his Bokken and they perform Ichi Kotae.

M

DOBARAI UCHI: 胴払打

Uke goes to Hasso no Kamae, paces forward and comes to Chudan no Kamae. At the same time Tori comes to Honte no Kamae and both are at right posture, and the Bokken and Jo are just crossing.

A

B

C

D

E

F

Uke brings the Bokken back to left Hasso in an effort to cut past the Jo and in the direction of Tori's right hip. As he does so Tori paces back with his right foot, into a slight side on stance and slides his right hand to the top end of the Jo. The left hand remains where it is and palms the Jo so the grip is reversed. The left hand then slides up the Jo to a point that is level with Tori's left shoulder, and the arms are extended straight. The Jo is level but sloping down, with the parallel plain of Tori's body, who is now standing in a side on stance. This movement is made by Tori as the cut is made, so that the outside of the tip of the Jo, blocks the impact of the cut from Uke.

Tori's right hand draws the Jo up through the left hand, until the end is back in the palm of the left hand. As the left hand changes to normal grip so the right hand slides back down the Jo and strikes directly down on the Bokken, knocking it towards the floor, the feet remain as they are, with the left foot forward. As the Jo comes up again from the strike so Tori steps forward with his right foot and brings the tip of the Jo to Uke's eyes.

Uke adjusts his position so the Bokken and the Jo tip cross and repeats his cut. The technique continues to the end of the dojo and both remain with the Bokken and Jo tips crossing.

G

H

I

J

TAIHAZUSHI UCHI (MIGI):

右休外打

Keeping the same positions Uke goes to Hasso Kamae with his left foot forward. When this happens Tori, who is in Honte no Kamae with the right foot forward, draws the Jo back to its full extent with the left hand but the right remains where it is. The right hand is now placed on the right knee and the left hand extends up and to the left, so that it is level with the left shoulder. Both the arms are straight and the Jo runs between the two hands, and at an angle from left to right sloping downwards. Here Tori waits.

Uke now cuts down towards Tori's head and steps forward with the right foot. As the cut comes, Tori brings his right foot to his left, and at the same time brings his left forearm parallel over his forehead. The Jo runs vertical down the right side of the body and slides through the right hand so that the right hand is straight by the right side of the body and holding the Jo loosely. In a big downward strike from this position the Jo hits the extended Bokken in a sweeping movement, knocking it downwards and at the same time steps back with the left foot. From here the Jo comes up to the eyes.

A

B

C

D

70

Uke steps forward into Hasso no Kamae with his left foot and Tori comes to Honte no Kamae, right foot forward. Uke comes to forward with his right foot and again cuts to the head and the technique is repeated to the end of the dojo. Uke and Tori are now in right posture with the tips of the Bokken and Jo crossing, Uke lowers the Bokken and paces to the left, then they perform Ichi Kotae.

E

F

G

H

I

J

71

TAIHAZUSHI UCHI (Hidari):

左体外打

Uke takes up Hasso Kamae and advances to Tori, who comes into Hidari Honte no Kamae (left honte no kamae). To do this he advances his left leg and at the same time grips the Jo above the right hand and slides the right hand to the end of the Jo, bringing the Jo forward and pointing at Uke's eyes. Uke brings the Bokken to Chudan and crosses the Jo as before, then advances his left foot into Hasso no Kamae.

The technique is now a mirror image of the previous one, from Tori's point of view. The right hand slides the Jo back to its full extent, then the left hand places the end of the Jo on the left knee, while the right hand extends in line with the right shoulder. Uke advances his right leg and again cuts at Tori's head. Tori brings his right forearm above his head as he steps back with his left foot to his right, the Jo slides vertical along his left side, with the left hand extended and relaxed at his side. The hands do not change their grip for either of these techniques, in this way he just avoids the cut.

A

B

C

D

Tori now makes a big downward strike at the Bokken, knocking it to Uke's left side. Then follows the Jo up to Uke's eyes and advances his left foot, with the Jo still in Hidari Honte no Kamae. As the strike comes to the Bokken, Uke paces back, allowing the Bokken to go to his left side then advances his left foot into Hasso no Kamae. Tori again makes the first two moves with the Jo, as before, leaving his head vulnerable and the technique is repeated.

At the end of the dojo Uke ends in Chudan no Kamae and Tori in Honte no Kamae. Both return to their original respective positions and Uke puts the Bokken to his left side. Tori lowers the Jo in Tsune no Kamae. Uke lowers the Bokken from his hip and Tori lowers the Jo to Sake Jo, then both exponents bow to each other having completed the Jodo Kihon.

E

F

G

H

I

74

ZEN NIHON KENDO RENMEI SEITEI JODO GATA

In this section I will describe the Kata, but to appreciate the training let me first mention Kata itself. Kata means form in English, but it is not just the repetition of techniques, that would be boring and shallow. To get the most from Kata it must reflect the deeper spirit of the training, each step must be of individual significance and not just a whole jumble of movements running into each other.

In Kata both Uke and Tori are working together in harmony, but this does not mean being soft and insipid. Each part of the Kata is a response to an attack and as such the attack should be done with intention and determination. The reason there is no injury lies in the fact that the response to the attack is performed with equal intention and determination. In this respect the exponents should exhibit fighting spirit. If one of the exponents sets out to do something other than the movements of the Kata, so he can catch out his adversary or show him up, then this is not Kata and the whole process becomes destructive to both individuals.

The Kata is a means of perfecting technique and perfecting self, through the correct understanding of technique. I remember the words of the maxim that stood above the door of the London Judo Society when it was in Vauxhall, London, in 1957, it read: 'Sport to win, sport to lose, in skill opposed, in spirit united', these words reflect the rapport you need with your opponent.

In the Jodo Seitei No Kata there are twelve sequences, which are Jo against Bokken and are in the order of practice:

75

TSUKIZUE 着杖

Uke and Tori face each other and bow, Uke goes to Hasso no Kamae. Tori goes from Tsune no Kamae, reaching his right hand forward and resting the bottom of the Jo about one foot ahead of a centre line between the two feet. The right hand slides to the top of the Jo, which is vertical with the ground.

A

B

C

D

E

F

Uke approaches Tori in Hasso no Kamae and pauses with his left foot forward, with a step forward of the right foot he cuts at Tori's head. Tori retreats his right foot to his rear right corner and allows the stick to lean at an angle in that direction at the same time the right hand palms the top of the stick and reverses his grip over the top. The left hand holds the stick so that both hands are in the position they would be in Honte. This action is to avoid the cut that Uke has just made, and is done as the sword comes down.

Uke is now in Chudan after the first cut so Tori takes advantage of this, raises the stick up and strikes down at Ukes left wrist, pacing forward as he does so.

Uke now steps his right foot back to Jodan no Kamae and as he is going back, Tori keeps his left hand where it is and slides the Jo back with his right hand so that the forward tip goes into his left hand. Then palming the Jo he steps forward with his right foot and both hands slide over the ends of the Jo and he strikes at Ukes raised left wrist sliding the Jo through his right hand.

As Uke lowers the Bokken, Tori lowers the Jo and stops it at Ukes eyes.

He then performs Osamekata once the Bokken has been lowered. To do this he keeps his right hand where it is and slides the Jo back with his left hand, when the Jo tip is in the right palm Tori places his right hand on his right knee, still holding the Jo. This is the same type of movement as Taihazushi Uchi. The right hand now changes its grip so that the palm is now facing the knee, the left hand remains the same. The Jo now slides through the right hand into Tsune no Kamae at the right side. The left hand slides from the Jo to the left side. Uke retreats.

A

B

C

D

A

B

C

D

E

F

SUIGETSU:  水月

Tori remains in Tsune no Kamae, Uke goes to Hasso no Kamae. Uke advances towards Tori, pauses with the left foot forward and then cuts to the head. As the cut comes down Tori advances his right foot to his right front corner and turns his body anticlockwise so he is side on and the Bokken just passes him, to do this the left foot also moves a little. In this same movement Tori also brings his left hand to his left hip, placing his palm flat against his body. The right hand brings the Jo into Uke's solar plexus as it slides from the hip.

Uke now steps back to Hasso no Kamae and at the same time Tori steps back with the right foot and comes into Hikiotoshi no Kamae. Uke advances his right foot and presents the Bokken in Chudan no Kamae as a threat or challenge to Tori. Tori strikes the Bokken with Hikiotoshi, sending it to Uke's right side. The tip of the Jo comes directly up to Uke's eyes and then Tori performs Osamekata in the same manner as the last technique. Uke retreats.

A

B

C

D

HISSAGE: 引提

Uke advances his left foot and goes into Hasso no Kamae. Tori takes a side on posture, with the left foot forward. The top of the Jo is lowered and the right hand turned anticlockwise so that the palm is facing outwards and the back of the hand rests against the outside thigh of the right leg. In doing this the stick rests along the outside of the leg and up behind the arm, so that it is concealed from Uke's sight.

Uke advances towards Tori, but before he gets within cutting distance Tori pivots his right hip forward so that the top half of the Jo slips from the hip and points towards Uke's eyes. Tori then brings his right foot up to his left and extends the rest of the Jo forward, the right hand still holding it in reverse grip. At this point Tori grips the end of the Jo with his left hand in the normal manner and steps back with his left foot. As the Jo is coming forward Uke advances his right foot and crosses the Jo in Chudan no Kamae.

A

B

C

D

Uke advances his left foot and goes into Hidare Jodan and Tori paces back and takes the Jo so that it runs diagonally down his left side. The hands remain in the same grip, the right hand is palm out and the knuckles are against the chest. The left hand is knuckles out and holds the Jo a short way below the left hip.

Uke advances his right foot and cuts to the head, as he does this Tori advances his right foot to his right front corner and his left foot forward, at the same time bringing the Jo above his head in Kuritsuke. The tip of the Jo raises to the Tsuka and Tori paces forward trapping Ukes hands and Bokken against the front of his body.

E

F

G

Uke begins to move away from the Jo, facing towards Tori as he does so. Tori turns his hips towards Uke, releases his left hand and takes a normal grip on the Jo. Tori pushes Uke in the solar plexus with the tip of the Jo as he moves away. Tori steps his right foot back and assumes Hikiotoshi no Kamae, then advances forward with his right foot and performs the action of Hikiotoshi, bringing the Jo to Uke's eyes. Uke however has not this time presented the Bokken and the Hikiotoshi is a means of driving him back and gaining control. Tori then performs Osamekata as before described.

Note: As Uke is thrust in the solar plexus, he should already be pacing back to absorb the shock, and should not stand and wait for it. Then he takes a further pace back as Tori does Hikiotoshi, but the Bokken is not raised.

H   **I**

SHAMEN:

Uke goes to Hasso no Kamae and advances his left foot, then he advances towards Tori, who remains in Tsune no Kamae. As Uke begins to cut at Tori's head, Tori brings his left hand to the front tip of the Jo and takes hold in reverse grip. As the cut comes down Tori steps his right foot to his right front corner and the left foot to the right, so that he avoids the cut. At the same time he swings the Jo from his hip, in a sideways action from right to left and strikes the top end of the Jo at Uke's left temple (make sure you do not hit the target by accident).

Uke goes back with his right foot to Hidare Jodan. Tori pivots on his right foot, keeps his left hand where it is and performs right Kaeshizuke against Ukes solar plexus. This time Uke does not move back, but remains in Jodan until Tori brings the tip of the Jo to his eyes, then after a pause he paces back and lowers the Bokken.

A

B

C

85

D

E

F

G

Tori is in left Honte no Kamae and to perform Osamekata he draws the Jo back with his right hand to its full extension. Brings his left hand to his advanced left knee and rests the knuckles against it. The Jo is now diagonally between the left knee and the right hand, which is extended parallel with the ground and level with the right shoulder. Tori changes his left hand so that it is now on top of the Jo and knuckles facing outwards, then the right hand changes grip over the top of the Jo so that the palm is facing outwards. The left hand places the end of the Jo to the right side of the body, just below the right hip. The right hand slides down the Jo to about half way and the left hand allows the Jo to slide through it into Tsune no Kamae. The right foot comes up to the left and the left hand returns to the left side.

SAKAN: 左貫

Uke comes to Hasso no Kamae with his left foot advanced. Tori comes to the same Kamae as for Tsukihazushi Uchi, that is with the Jo parallel to the floor and above his head, the feet are spread apart. Uke advances and pauses just out of Maiai (combative distance). As with Tsukihazushi Uchi, he draws the sword to his left hip in the same manner, with the left foot remaining forward. Uke then advances his right foot and makes a thrust at Tori's left side. Tori deflects the blade in the same manner as Taihazushi Uchi and strikes the sword away, then takes two paces forward driving the end of the Jo in the direction of Uke's eyes. Uke steps back to avoid the thrusts. From this point in the technique it varies from that of Tsukihazushi Uchi. Uke steps back to Hasso no Kamae, with his left foot advanced and Tori steps back with his right foot into Hikiotoshi no Kamae.

A

B

C

D

Uke steps forward with his right foot into Chudan no Kamae, in a rather challenging posture. Tori steps forward with his right foot and strikes the Bokken to Uke's right side, with Hikiotoshi, then brings the Jo up to Uke's eyes. From here Tori performs right Osamekata.

E

F

G

H

I

J

MONOMI:

Tori is in Tsune no Kamae, the left hand holds the Jo palm up, just in front of the right hand.
The Jo is brought across the front of the body to the left and parallel with it by the left hand,
until the right hand holds the end of the Jo. The Jo is then lowered so the other end is on the
floor past the left side of the body and the Jo runs at an angle from the right hand downwards.
Uke is in Hasso no Kamae as before and advances towards Tori.

E

F

Uke pauses with his left foot forward, then cuts to the head. Tori steps to his left rear corner with his left foot and brings the Jo up into his left hand the right foot steps backwards to the left rear corner and goes up behind the left foot. In this way Tori is to Uke's right front corner and has avoided the cut. As Tori makes the avoidance step with his right foot the Jo comes forward and down onto Uke's right wrist.

Uke steps his right foot back to Jodan no Kamae and at the same time Tori pivots on his left foot, keeps his right hand where it is and performs left Kaeshizuke at Uke's solar plexus. Uke does not move and after the thrust, Tori brings the tip of the Jo to Uke's eyes. Uke lowers the Bokken and paces back a little, Tori does Osamekata.

G

H

I

91

KASUMI: 霞

Tori is in Tsune no Kamae and takes the end of the Jo with his left hand in reverse position. He goes into left posture bringing the Jo above his head so that the last foot or so is at head height. The left hand is about a foot and a half in front of the centre of the chest and the Jo is sloping back over the head. The right hand is open and the palm is facing outward and a little in front of the forehead. This Kamae is to help you see on a strong sunny day or in a mist, when you have poor vision through the elements.

A

B

C

D

Uke is in Hasso no Kamae and advances towards Tori, he pauses and both Uke and Tori come to Chudan and cross weapons, Tori is in right Gyakute no Kamae as he lowers the Jo.

Tori draws the Jo back with his left hand to its full extent but does not palm the Jo. Tori steps forward with his left foot and at the same time slides the Jo forward and through his left hand, striking the Bokken in a slicing action and knocking it to Uke's left side. Uke paces the strike back to his left side, then steps back with his right foot to Hasso no Kamae. Tori keeps the Jo to his eyes until he has stepped back, then paces back in the same posture, bringing the Jo to his right side in a side on posture. The hands have still not changed grip on the Jo but it is now diagonally across the body, with the left hand palm out and holding it to the chest. The right hand is a little below hip level and the palm is facing inwards.

Uke again steps forwards to cut the head, Tori advances his right leg and at the same time brings the Jo up to the Tsuka, above his head. Uke brings his feet together and at the same time brings his left hand above the left side of the head and the right above the right. The Bokken is now parallel to the floor and above Uke's head. This is an attempt on Uke's part to swing the sword round and get a cut at Tori's neck. As Uke makes this move, Tori performs Dobarai Uchi and pushes Uke backwards.

F

H

I

J

K

L

Uke paces off the force of the push and goes to Hasso no Kamae with the left foot forward. Tori paces back into a side on posture with his right foot forward. The Jo is held with the same grip but slides his hands to the other end of the Jo and the right hand at the chest, holding the end of the Jo at chest level, with the knuckles towards the chest. The left hand is about hip level with the palm facing outwards.

Uke advances his right foot and cuts at the head. As the cut comes, Tori steps his right foot to his right front corner and advances his left foot, the Jo comes up to the tsuka and Tori does Kuritsuke. The sword is trapped against Uke's body, on the left side.

N

P

As Uke begins to move away from the hold on the Bokken, at the point where he is moving back but facing Tori, Tori changes his left hand grip to a normal grip and turns his hips towards Uke, thrusting to the solar plexus as he does so. Uke paces back from the thrust and as he does so Tori goes to right Hikiotoshi no Kamae, advances his right foot and drives towards Uke with Hikiotoshi. Uke does not raise the Bokken, but paces back, Tori stops with the Jo directed at Uke's eyes. Tori performs Osamekata and ends as usual in Tsune no Kamae.

TACHIOTOSHI: 太刀落

Uke begins in Hasso no Kamae and Tori in Tsune no Kamae, Uke advances towards Tori but before he reaches cutting distance, Tori grips the end of the Jo with the left hand in reverse and at the same time steps back with the right foot. Uke begins to come to Chudan no Kamae and Tori retreats the left foot and at the same time brings the Jo in a big overhead movement to Chudan, and crosses the Bokken. The right hand of Tori is in reverse grip.

A

B

C

D

E

F

G

H

Tori paces his right foot across the front of the left foot a little and at the same time draws the Jo back to its full extent with the left hand. This takes Tori out of line from the point of Uke's Bokken tip. Tori now steps forward with his left foot towards Uke and at the same time, slides his left hand back down the Jo while he strikes at Uke's right head with the extended end. The hands do not change position so the left hand is now in reverse grip and the right in normal grip.

I

J

K

L

As the strike comes at Uke, he raises the Bokken in the same manner he does for Dobarai Uchi. That is with the Bokken above the head parallel to the ground and the point facing the right, this is done to block the strike. Uke then advances his left leg to his front left corner, a little and tries to cut at the right side of Tori's neck, in a clockwise direction from its present position.

Tori defends against the cut by sliding the left hand to the far end of the Jo and at the same time bringing it above his head, the right hand also slides to the far end of the Jo as it slides up under the attacking Bokken, and strikes under the Tsuka. The feet remain the same during this movement, and the hands do not change their grip. Tori now steps forward with his right foot and does Kuritsuke, trapping Uke's hand and Bokken to the front of his body, to his right side.

Uke begins to back away from Tori and at the same time to face him. As this happens Tori pivots his right foot to his right, raises the Jo and brings it over to his right side, palming it through his left hand as he does so. He is now in a position to do Kaeshizuke, he steps forward with his left foot and thrusts at Uke's solar plexus.

Uke steps back to avoid the impact of the thrust, at the same time Tori paces back with his right foot, into Hikiotoshi no Kamae. Tori advances his right foot and does Hikiotoshi, stopping at Uke's eyes. Uke does not raise his Bokken but takes a pace back to avoid the strike. Tori then does Osamekata.

RAIUCHI: 雷打

Uke advances his left foot to Hasso no Kamae, Tori who is in Tsune no Kamae brings the Jo into the same starting Kamae he did for Kasumi. The Jo is above the head, with the right hand open as if to shade the eyes and the left hand holding the end of the Jo.

Before Uke comes to within cutting distance, both Uke and Tori Chudan no Kamae. Tori's right hand is holding the Jo with reverse grip. Uke paces forward with his right foot and with a big cutting action tries to cut at Tori's left side. Tori paces forward with his right foot as the cut is made, and at the same time raises the Jo above his head and thrusts the tip in Uke's solar plexus. The Jo is sloping down from above the head and apart from getting its target, the lower end also blocks Uke's wrists and prevents the cut.

A

B

C

D

100

E

F

G

H

Uke brings his right foot back to his left, then advances his left foot and having drawn the Bokken above his head, tries to cut at Tori's right side. Tori brings his right foot to his left foot and slides his right hand to the far end of the Jo, then advances his left foot and at the same time thrusts the other end of the Jo across Uke's right side, towards the solar plexus. As he does this the left hand slides to the far end of the Jo, which is above Tori's head in the same manner the technique was performed on the right.

I

Uke moves slowly away from the Jo and as he does so Tori keeps light pressure, eventually pointing the tip of the Jo at Uke's eyes. Tori's left hand is in reverse grip on the Jo, he changes it to normal grip and performs left Osamekata.

SEIGAN:

正眼

A　　　　　　　　　　　　　　　　　　　　　　　　　**B**

Tori is in Tsune no Kamae and Uke has the Bokken at his left hip, both advance towards each other. Uke reaches his right hand to the Tsuka in an action of going to draw the sword. As this happens Tori advances his right foot and raises the Jo forward to Uke's eyes, the left hand grips the end of the Jo as it goes from the eyes, to the top of the right wrist and traps Uke's hands as he grasps the Tsuka. Uke pauses and then he steps back with his right foot, at the same time drawing his Bokken directly back above the right side of his head with the tip facing that direction, this is a big flourish movement. Tori takes advantage of this situation and as Uke is going back, he turns his right foot to the right, draws his right hand up the Jo into Gyakute Uchi no Kamae. Tori steps forward with his left foot and thrusts in Gyakute at Uke's solar plexus, the strike makes contact.

Uke grips the end of the Tsuka with his left hand, advances his right foot and makes a cut from Tori's left shoulder to his right hip. As the cut comes, Tori pulls his left hand sharply to his stomach and at the same time brings his left foot back to the right. The right hand comes to the right shoulder, so the Jo is vertical. Tori now advances his right foot, after the Bokken has completed it's cut, and strikes across Uke's chest with the end of the Jo. Tori now comes to Uke's eyes and then to Osamekata.

C

D

E

F

G

MIDAREDOME:

Uke comes to Hasso no Kamae, Tori is again in Tsune no Kamae and steps back with his right foot to a side on posture. Tori then places the Jo behind the right leg and back in the same manner he did for Hissage.

A

B

As Uke advances in Hasso no Kamae, Tori turns his hips forward and lets the Jo come forward and at the same time brings his right foot to his left. He grips the end of the Jo with his left hand and steps back with the left foot. He is now in Chudan Kamae with the tip crossing the Bokken, because at the same time Uke comes to Chudan Kamae with the Bokken. Tori has his right foot forward and the right hand is in reverse grip. So far the opening of this technique is the same as Hissage. Tori now draws the Jo back with his left hand, to its full extent, then advancing the left foot, strikes down at the right side of Uke's Bokken. To do this the left hand slides down the Jo as that end reaches forward for the strike. The Jo points at Uke's eyes as he takes the force of the strike, drawing the Bokken back to his left side and pacing backwards.

D

E

F

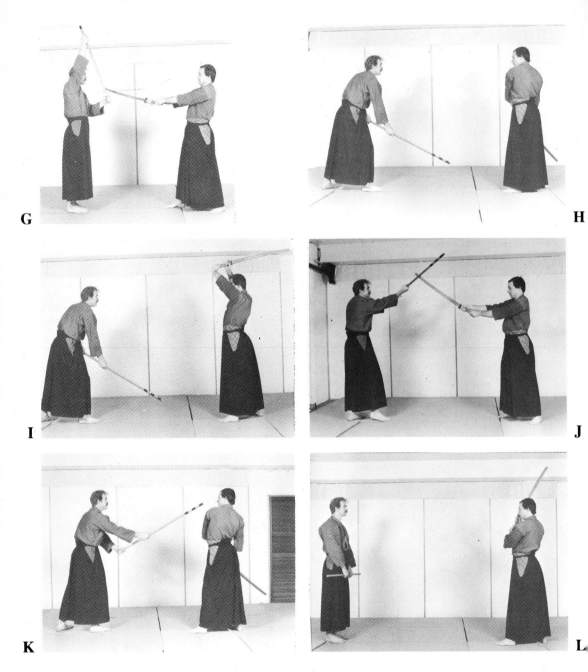

G

H

I

J

K

L

Uke goes to Hasso no Kamae and advances his right foot to cut at Tori's left neck. As Uke goes back, Tori has himself paced back and brought the Jo to his right side, in a side on stance, the stance is the same as that taken for Kuritsuke, but as the cut comes Tori brings his right foot up to his left and brings the Jo over his head and to his left side of his body, so that the tip threatens Uke's eyes. Neither hand has changed position and the right hand is still in reverse grip. The Jo is in a line close to the Bokken and thus preventing any further continuance of the cut.

Tori keeps tension on his reversed right hand, then stepping back with his left leg, he releases his grip with the left hand. The Jo spins upwards and he catches the other end of the Jo with the left hand, in a normal grip. This movement is done in a fraction of a second and Tori with the Jo in a Honte like Kamae, strikes down on the left side of the Bokken, sweeping it to Uke's right side.

Uke uses the momentum of the strike and continues the circle back over his head, at the same time drawing his right foot back to his left. Then in the same movement bringing the right foot forward again and cutting down at Tori's head. Tori, still holding the Jo in right Honte, brings his right foot back to his left and draws the cut up with Makiotoshi. Then again advances his right foot and sweeps Uke's blade down to Uke's right side. The Jo then comes up to the eyes in a forward thrust, Tori takes another step and again drives Uke back with a thrust at the eyes. Uke paces back on both occasions.

Q

R

S

T

As Uke goes to Hasso no Kamae, so Tori advances his left foot to his right he releases his left hand grip on the Jo and allows it to run level with his body and vertical to the ground, at about groin height. The left hand again takes hold of the Jo directly on the left side of the right hand, with the knuckles facing in the same direction, both hands in the centre and the centre in line with the centre of the body. Uke advances his right foot and cuts to the centre of the head. Tori slides his left hand to the rear end of the Jo, as he advances his right foot and at the same time raises the Jo forward above his head, so that the other end of the Jo is across Uke's left side of the Tsuka, and the tip pointing at Uke's eyes.

Uke brings the right foot back to the left and raises the Bokken above his head in the same manner as Dobarai Uchi. Tori steps forward with the left foot to the right and pushes Uke back in Dobarai Uchi. As Uke goes back, Tori paces his right foot back into Hikiotoshi no Kamae. Uke again steps forward with his right foot, from Hasso no Kamae and presents his Bokken in Chudan no Kamae, as a challenge. Tori advances his right foot as he does Hikiotoshi and follows the strike to Uke's eyes. Uke's Bokken is at his right side, as before, he retreats a little. Tori is in right Honte and now does Osamekata.

108

RANAI:

Uke has the Bokken at his side and Tori is in Tsune no Kamae, both advance towards each other. Uke pauses with his right foot forward and brings his right hand to the Tsuka, at the same time Tori advances his right foot and raises the Jo to Uke's eyes. In the same movement Tori grips the Jo directly under his right hand, in normal grip and at the same time brings his left foot to his right. Tori now slides his right hand to the top end of the Jo and over, at the same time the left foot advances and the lower end of the Jo is placed in Uke's right side. This action prevents Uke from drawing the Bokken or moving in at Tori.

Uke steps back with his right foot and draws the sword in a big flourish over the left side of his head, with the point in that direction. Tori paces back into the right side on posture he takes for Kuritsuke, which is with the left foot forward and the Jo coming down at an angle from his left chest. The hands do not change but slide to the other end of the Jo as he goes back.

1

2

3

4

Uke advances his right foot and cut at the head. Tori extends the hands and brings the Jo tip at Uke's eyes, then steps forward with the right foot. In the same movement Tori pivots anticlockwise, taking his left foot to his rear as he turns, and brings the other end of the Jo under the Tsuka. Tori is now on the left side of Uke, facing in the same direction and with the Jo on the same plain as Uke. Tori now leans a little backwards and in a rising circular motion in his direction, draws Uke's hands and Bokken over his head and traps them against Uke's body, on Uke's left side.

5

6

7

8

Uke tries to get a cut in at Tori's side by bringing the Bokken back to his left side and pacing in that direction, then advancing forward again one pace and cutting at Tori's right side. As Uke paces back Tori paces into him and at the same time slides his right hand down the Jo to the tip, which he keeps at Uke's body. The right hand goes to the other end of the Jo and palms over the top. Both of Tori's feet are together and as Uke makes his cut, Tori turns clockwise 180 degrees and slides his left hand up the Jo so that the end goes into Uke's side and wedges against Uke's arms preventing the cut.

10

12

Uke moves back and again goes to Hasso no Kamae. Tori paces back and changes the left hand grip on the Jo so that he is in the position he was earlier for Kuritsuke, which is side on posture with the left foot forward.

Uke advances and cuts to Tori's left neck. As the cut comes Tori advances the right foot and brings the lower end of the Jo upwards and forwards to Uke's eyes. The right hand, which is in reverse grip, keeps tension on the Jo. The left hand releases its grip and that end spins upwards, the left hand grasps the other end. In the same movement Tori strikes down with the top end of the Jo at the Bokken. As the Bokken is struck down to Uke's right side, he steps back with his right foot, keeps the momentum going, advances the right foot again and brings the Bokken over his head and cuts to Tori's head. Tori slides his right hand up the Jo and over the top, as he raises that end above his head. The left hand slides up the Jo as Tori advances his left foot and that end comes up under the downward cut, before it gets too deep, and ends up with the lower tip in Uke's right side and the shaft of the Jo blocking the arms of the downward cut.

13

14

15

16

Uke and Tori retreat from each other, Uke goes to Hasso no Kamae and Tori paces back to Hikiotoshi no Kamae sliding the Jo through his hands as he does so. Tori then advances his right foot and strikes at Uke with a Hikiotoshi movement towards his head. Uke blocks this with the blocking surface of the Bokken near the hilt, the Bokken tip is facing to the right side of Uke. Uke pushes against the Jo and Tori resists, in this fashion they take two paces forward but on the third pace Tori releases his pressure and Uke takes advantage of it by advancing his left foot and making a slash across Tori's stomach, from left to right. Tori steps back with his right foot, slides his right hand to the far end of the Jo and as he does so raises the Jo above his head but in front of it, so the tip in the left hand is pointing at Uke's eyes. As the cut passes Tori changes both hand grips by palming the Jo at either end, lowers the Jo to waist level on his right side and thrusts to Uke's solar plexus, pushing him back.

7

18

9

20

Uke walks off the thrust and goes to Hasso no Kamae. Tori paces back to a right side on posture, with the left leg forward, the Jo comes to the ready position for Kuritsuke and left hand changes its grip at the top of the Jo, so the knuckles are facing the chest. Uke advances his right foot and cuts to the head. Tori steps his left foot to his front left corner and advances the right foot, as he does this he brings the Jo up under the Tsuka and does right Kurihanashi on Uke.

Uke paces off the power of the technique and ends with his left foot towards Tori but his body facing away from Tori, the Bokken having been knocked past Uke's right side. Uke again takes hold of the end of the Tsuka with his left hand after it has been released by the power of the Jo technique. Uke's. Keeping his feet where they are, Uke turns his body towards Tori in an anti clockwise direction and at the same time brings the Bokken over his head in a large arc to his left hip. Uke then steps forward with his right foot towards Tori and at the same time thrusts the Bokken forward to drive him back. Until this moment Tori has kept the Jo in the direction of Uke's eyes but now he steps back with his right foot into Hikiotoshi Kamae, changing the grip of his right hand as he does so.

21   22

23   24

Tori then steps back with the left foot and comes to Honte no Kamae in a striking action and drives Uke back two paces. On the third pace Uke begins to draw the Bokken back to Hasso no Kamae, at that moment Tori steps forward with the Jo in a swinging action, bringing it down past his right side back over his head and forward again to Uke's eyes.

Uke is now in Hasso no Kamae and advances his right foot in an effort to cut across Tori's stomach, this time from Tori's left to right. Tori raises the Jo, still pointing at Uke's eyes and draws his right foot to his left, letting the cut pass through, with the Jo raised well above Tori's head. As the slash passes, Tori advances his right foot and brings the Jo to Uke's solar plexus between the two hands holding the Bokken.

25

26

27

28

Uke withdraws a pace from the Jo and tries to cut at Tori's right side, by bringing the Bokken back to his left, advancing forward again and cutting. As this happens Tori steps back with his right foot and slides his hands to the other end of the Jo in the manner of Dobarai Uchi, that means the left hand palms the end nearest Uke as Tori paces back. Tori blocks the cut with Dobarai Uchi. Tori then strikes down at the Bokken, in the same manner as Dobarai Uchi. Uke avoids this by stepping well back with his right foot and going to Hasso no Kamae. Uke then cuts at the exposed head of Tori, but as the cut comes down, Tori strikes the right side of Uke's Bokken in an upward sweep and at the same time brings the right foot back to the left and the Jo comes to almost vertical and at the right side of the chest after it has struck the Bokken to Uke's left side. Tori then advances his right foot again and brings the end of the Jo down across Uke's chest. Uke lowers the Jo and faces forward. Tori comes to Uke's eyes and then ends with Osamekata. Both return to their original positions, Uke brings the Bokken to his side, Tori lowers the Jo to Sage Jo, both bow and this concludes the 12 kata.

29

30

31

32

33

Guests at the reception given on the presentation of the Emperors Award to Shimizu Dai Sensei for his contributions to martial arts in Japan.

Shimizu Dai Sensei 25th and last Grand Master of Shindo Muso Ryu Jojutsu.

Shimizu Dai Sensei (right) during a moment of free time during a display with the present authority on Shindo Muso Ryu Jojutsu, Ichitaro Kuroda Sensei.

117

Donn F. Draeger Sensei (left) and Quintin Chambers (right).

Tsunemori Kaminoda Sensei (right).

JODO AND JOJUTSU,
PAST PRESENT AND FUTURE

I think it is first of all important to remember that the techniques in this book are Kendo Remmei Seitei JODO and were taken as a very small number of representative techniques, from the original style of SHINDO MUSO RYU JOJUTSU. These techniques are NOT Shindo Muso Ryu, per se.

The study of traditional Martial Arts was very much a closed shop for foreigners who studied in Japan after the last war. To get to the root of the Martial Art spirit, to know the minds of past masters, to experience what existed in the time of the Bushi (Samurai), was hidden beneath the surface of the more modern systems. Right down to modern times the Japanese Masters in Classical Martial Art systems, have feared the commercial approach to such skills. Often in the Modern systems emphasis is put on attaining grade, over and above the·development of skill and the deeper understanding of the principles. Who can blame the masters for their judgement, when we look at the 'Martial Arts' that have been influenced by the Western World.

The old systems contained much within their skills, that were transmitted by direct experience. The masters would work on a one to one basis with each student, thus allowing his character and experience to flow into the training session and through the technique, into his student. This can never be achieved in a large class. When the time was ready, certain secrets of the training would be passed on in the way described, the understanding would grow within the student and in this way his study would be a complete one.

Were it not for the work of one man, I doubt if Westerners in Japan would ever have been able to do more than scratch the surface of classical Martial Arts study. That man was Donn F. Draeger, who alone took over 40 years to gain the confidence and respect of Japan's great Masters and through this made it possible for others to follow in his footsteps and get a glimpse of the hidden side of these skills. It was through his efforts that it was possible for people such as myself to be accepted as part of a traditional Martial Arts school. There was in this field of study no greater exponent, more dedicated or qualified or more capable of representing Martial Arts as they really are. Donn F. Draeger was born in 1922 and passed away in October 1982. He was author of many books, that I would recommend to those who never knew him, as factual and foremost in their field.

The last grand master of SHINDO MUSO RYU JOJUTSU was Takaji Shimizu dai sensei, when he passed on some ten years ago, he did not designate another grand master. This is for reasons that I will not enter into in this book, but as a result of this action the true teachings of Shindo Muso Ryu and the true line of descent ended with him. Twenty-five generations of grand masters have ended in this the 20th century, it is a sad loss of cultural heritage.

With the passing of Donn F. Draeger, it became a little more difficult for foreigners in Japan to study the style of Shindo Muso Ryu Jojutsu and doors began to close. Their direction was uncertain as you will understand as you read on.

Many of Shimizu Dai Sensei's senior teachers went towards their own direction and as a result of this action, the original style has been subject to personal changes. This in itself is not a wrong action in respect of the seniority of those who have effected the changes, however a situation has now come about where correct action in one dojo, may not be correct in another, as a result of a teacher's personal changes.

The growth of variation in original form moves the development of Jo further away from its original source and in this way tradition becomes, step by step, modern form. It is hard to say where the final direction of this trend will end but I feel sure it will be away from the source from which it started. This however is conjecture, what is important is that the reader can see the importance of the position of grand master in a ryu, and in his passing the manner in which subtle changes begin to occur.

The person who began and remained with Shimizu Dai Sensei through his life time, and who was always seen to be working with him at every demonstration of the skill of Jojutsu, was Ichitaro Kuroda Sensei. He alone was the nearest person to him and the nearest to the original form, Kuroda Sensei is in Japan's mainland the most senior instructor in Shindo Muso Ryu Jojutsu. He has almost half a century of Jojutsu experience behind him and is perhaps the most respected person in his field. Kuroda Sensei was awarded the Emperor's medal for his contribution to Martial Arts in Japan. Among the students of Kuroda Sensei who have themselves become senior teachers are, Tsunemori Kaminoda and Hiroi Tsunetsugu.

There are now many organisations in respect of both Jojutsu and Jodo, for example the Kendo Remmei, International Jodo Federation, and the Shindo Muso Ryu. Each of these have a separate and independent grading system and in respect of the Seitei Kata, a different syllabus. The standards and technical requirements vary within each organisation and it is possible to hold various grades in the same skill but through different organisations. How this will reflect on the future development of Jo we again must wait and see.

The System of Shindo Muso Ryu have returned to the old idea of Menkyo (Certificates) of competence. The first is Okuiri which is about the level of 4th Dan and the highest is Kaiden which is about the level of 9th Dan. However there are some foreigners such as myself, who were graded to dan rank by the Grand master himself, and were told that the standard of his grade was far higher than that of others, by him.

The future of Jo is I believe quite diverse. Many who do not want the complexity of the Ryu system, will follow the modern form of the 'do' system, with the representative techniques of the Kendo Remmei (As described in this book). Others will train in the revised form of the Shindo Muso Ryu, and some will try to search out the origins of its source. The direction of others is of course a matter of personal choice, but for myself I will continue to train as I was instructed by the last Grand Master Takaji Shimizu Dai Sensei and will continue to be advised by Ichitaro Kuroda Sensei, who is the foremost living authority on the traditional system. With continued training, my film of the last Grand Master and profuse notes taken while training directly under him, I have established that my direction is to retain the original and traditional form of Shindo Muso Ryu Jojutsu. In Britain and Ireland this is effected under the Independent Jojutsu Federation, an organisation dedicated to retaining the original form as taught by Shimizu Dai Sensei.

I hope this book has proved to be an instructive and informative work on the modern form. It is my wish that in the future I will be able to produce a book on the original form of Shindo Muso Ryu.

I believe that it is important that true Martial Arts survive yet another generation and that this book will help to perpetuate that idea. In this respect you need a stable mind, with power of flexibility. There is nothing that can be gained from outside a person, that does not at first come from within oneself. The true path is the path of truth, the cleaving of self deception. If you once see the beauty of a true diamond, and take it to your heart, no imitation will possess its radiance. The student should seek out the true way, that is the meaning of 'Do'.